George A. Romero: Interviews

Conversations with Filmmakers Series
Gerald Peary, General Editor

George A. Romero
INTERVIEWS

Edited by Tony Williams

University Press of Mississippi / Jackson

www.upress.state.ms.us

The University Press of Mississippi is a member
of the Association of American University Presses.

Copyright © 2011 by University Press of Mississippi
All rights reserved
Manufactured in the United States of America

First printing 2011
∞
Library of Congress Cataloging-in-Publication Data
Romero, George.
  George A. Romero : interviews / edited by Tony Williams.
      p. cm. — (Conversations with filmmakers series)
  Includes index.
  ISBN 978-1-61703-027-7 (cloth : alk. paper) — ISBN 978-1-61703-029-1 (pbk. : alk. paper)
— ISBN 978-1-61703-028-4 1. Romero, George A.—Interviews. 2. Motion picture producers
and directors—United States—Interviews. I. Williams, Tony. II. Title.
  PN1998.3.R644A3 2011
  791.4302'33092—dc22   2010052442

British Library Cataloging-in-Publication Data available

Contents

Introduction

The name of George A. Romero is inevitably associated with the zombie component of the American horror film, one that he pioneered in 1968 with his innovative black and white independent film production *Night of the Living Dead* and an arena within which he still works today. Ironically, George Romero began as an independent film director working within the commercial field in Pittsburgh and continues to this day over forty years later having relocated to Canada still contributing to the generic area which saw his emergence as director. However, Romero is no horror film director but an independent in every sense of the word wishing to transmit his unique vision to a field that is generally not taken seriously in American cinema and one which many of his former fans now think has left him behind.

However, despite the recent remakes of several classic Romero films over the past decade, Romero is far from being overshadowed by many of these misbegotten versions but still continues working within a genre that made him famous and contributing his distinctive touches to his recent work in the new millennium. This collection of interviews gathered from various sources is designed not only to let Romero speak for himself but also to reveal his endurance as a key creative figure over the past forty years. It is a mistake to regard him exclusively as a horror film director since he is really an independent social commentator on the American cultural and political landscape using the horror genre to make critical comments on a country that has deteriorated more rapidly than could have been imagined when he began his career.

This collection opens with one of the first of his published interviews conducted in one of the early issues of *Andy Warhol's Interview* where Romero speaks about his first venture in independent feature filmmaking and various production and distribution problems involved. He also mentions a forthcoming project whose working title was *At Home with the Angels* (later *There's Always Vanilla*) that would deal with contemporary youth culture, a subject far removed from his first film that would soon ironically become identified with him.

Romero is very much a product of the changes experienced in America during the 1960s, changes he has never entirely forgotten throughout his entire life and career. As he states in an April 23, 1979, *Village Voice* interview with Tom Allen appropriately titled "Knight of the Living Dead," "The world was just beginning to open up, and there was room for everybody. I did a gig on the school radio station and we had this outrageous format. I started to recognize, shit, this was what I wanted to do. It worked out, though a hell of a lot of people didn't give it a snowball's chance. As I'm telling you this story, I realize that way back then I had this incredible tenacity in terms of just everything I did. It was all moving in the same way. And I've been doing the same goddamn thing right through to today. And we do it now as a corporate philosophy. It's a matter of hanging on, whatever it takes."

He has the same philosophy years later still "hanging on" in Canada and seizing the opportunity to make his own type of cinema, one that reflects the same statement he made to Tom Allen when *Dawn of the Dead* erupted on to American cinema screens. "I don't want to make movies so that I can live in Hollywood. I don't want to make deals so that I can make movies. I want to make movies. Period."

The second interview conducted by Alex Ben Block for *Filmmakers Newsletter* investigates further the problems of independent film production affecting anyone existing outside the Hollywood mainstream, while the third interview for *Andy Warhol's Interview* clearly shows Romero's desire to make other films far different from the one that brought him to commercial and critical attention. In 1977 Romero eventually gains further critical attention as the interview by Dan Yakir in *Film Comment* shows where he speaks about his earlier films such as *There's Always Vanilla* and *Jack's Wife* as well as his plans for the future. With the release of *Dawn of the Dead* in 1979 aided by both Dario Argento and a new partnership, Romero contributes the second part of his zombie saga, one critiquing consumer capitalism that will soon become a characteristic feature of the new decade and the Reagan presidency. The September 1979 Toronto Film Festival interview shows an optimistic director at the pinnacle of his commercial success but also stressing that zombies are not the sole element of meaning in his films.

Although Romero is now becoming indelibly identified as the director of gory scary movies, he also wishes to stress that the monsters are really within us as the title of his 1981 *Rod Serling's The Twilight Zone* interview with Tom Seligson shows.

Following the commercial success of *Dawn of the Dead*, Romero takes on a very different film from those that seem to define him as a director, namely *Knightriders*. Dan Yakir's illuminating 1981 *American Film* interview reveals another side to the director's talent while the Hanners and Kloman interview from *Film Criticism* notes the director as social critic.

However, the commercial and critical failure of *Knightriders* and the relative success of *Creepshow* led Romero to return to his bleakest chapter in the zombie cycle so far—*Day of the Dead* (1985)—a grim indictment of the Reagan era and a film that has only recently gained the critical respect it deserves following its championship by Robin Wood in the same decade. Romero discusses this film in a 1985 interview with Paul Gagne while the other two interviews by Frederick Szebin and Dennis Fischer (also from *Cinefantastique*) outline Romero's feelings concerning *Monkey Shines*, future projects, and his increasing dissatisfaction with the Hollywood system he now finds himself associated with. However, critical respect for Romero and his work still continues as the 1992 interview with Stanley Wiater reveals.

At the end of the decade some light appears at the end of the tunnel as Romero turns his attention to filming in Canada with *Bruiser*. The new millennium begins with my 2000 interview that reveals new directions for Romero and further reflections on the past. "Let Them Eat Flesh," an interview prior to the release of the Universal production *Land of the Dead*, continues the coverage of this resilient talent by *Film Comment*.

Despite his status in North America, Romero has always been regarded as a major artistic talent as articles examining his work in foreign journals and two recent collections of essays—*Politique des Zombies* (2007) edited by Jean-Baptiste Thoret and *George A. Romero: Un Cinema Crepusculaire* (2008) edited by Frank Lafond—demonstrate.

Four interviews dealing with *Diary of the Dead* and *Survival of the Dead*, two recent Romero films, complete this collection: one by Beth Accomando, which has appeared on the Internet in an abbreviated form, two interviews by Peter Keough for the *Boston Phoenix*, and the most recent interview that I conducted specifically for this volume.

I wish to thank Leila Salisbury for agreeing to this project in place of the one she originally suggested as well as Kent Jones for helping me gain permission to reprint two interviews from *Film Comment*. Rusty

Nails, Suzy Desroches, Chris Weedman, and Brian Wilson contributed to this project in several ways. Valerie Jones and Mary Morris also made a monumental contribution by bringing this collection to completion.

TW

Chronology

1940   Born in the Bronx, New York City, on February 4.

1954   Begins filming on 8mm in the Scarsdale area of New York. Education at Suffield Academy, Connecticut.

1956   Shoots 8mm short productions, *Gorilla* and *Earthbottom*. Wins Future Scientists of America award for *Earthbottom*, a geology documentary made at Suffield.

1958   Begins studying art, design, and drama at Carnegie-Mellon Institute, Pittsburgh, Pennsylvania. Shoots 8mm short *Curly* and 16mm short *Slant*. Both are co-scripted with Rudolph J. Ricci.

1960   Begins work as an actor, director, and set painter in Pittsburgh.

1962   Completes work on first envisaged ambitious feature *Expostulations*, co-scripted with Rudolph J. Ricci. This was an anthology comprising several unrelated vignettes and satirical shorts such as "The Froomistan" about a mad scientist building a contraption in his backyard; "The Rocket Ship," dealing with a spaceship landing in an ice cream cone; "The Trilogy," viewing the experiences of a black in the ghetto; and "Door Against the Rain" about a boy finding his fantasy world outside his back door. Establishes TV production company "Latent Image" for industrial and commercial films. Shoots Latent Image Promotional Reel, a 16mm compilation short promoting the company and featuring fast-motion scenes of the crew at work. (During 1962–73, the Latent Image shoots thirty-second and sixty-second commercials for companies such as U.S. Steel, Calgon, Westinghouse, Koppers Inc., and H. J. Heinz. It also works on political campaign films such as *Lenore Romm*.)

1967   Co-directs and scripts *Screen Test* with Rudolph J. Ricci.

1968   Directs, photographs, and edits *Night of the Living Dead*, co-scripted with John A. Russo and based on a story by Romero. Image Ten Company is formed for feature production.

1970   Begins extensive work as TV director.

1972   Directs, photographs, and edits *There's Always Vanilla* (aka *The Affair* for southern drive-in circuits), scripted by Rudolph J. Ricci. The film is shot on 16mm color and blown up to 35mm. Working title, *At Play with the Angels*.

1973   Directs, photographs, edits, and scripts *Jack's Wife*. This 16mm color film is blown up to 35mm but reduced from its original running length of 130 minutes to 89 minutes by Jack Harris Enterprises for general distribution under the title *Hungry Wives*. It also circulates as *Season of the Witch*. Directs, edits, and scripts *The Crazies* (aka *Code Name Trixie*). Enters into partnership with Richard P. Rubinstein to form the Laurel Group.

1974   Directs *O. J. Simpson/Juice on the Loose* for *The Winners* series with Richard P. Rubinstein as producer and executive producer. Airs on ABC TV during December.

1975   Directs the following titles for *The Winners* "sports profile films" with Richard P. Rubinstein as producer and executive producer: *Reggie Jackson/One Man Bunch*; *Franco Harris/Good Luck on Sunday*; *NFL Films/The 27th Team*; *Bruno Sammartino/Strongman*; directs and produces *Tom Weiskopf/On Tour*; *Willie Stargell/If I Didn't Play Baseball*; *Johnny Rutherford/ Eleven Year Odyssey*. Co-executive producer with Richard P. Rubinstein of *Magic at the Roxy*, directed by Michael Gargulio on videotape. Producer/executive producer/co-producer and co-executive producer of the following "sports profile films" for the ABC TV syndicated series *The Winners* during Fall 1975 following *Monday Night Football*: *Kareem Abdul Jabbar/Nobody Roots for Goliath* directed by Richard P. Rubinstein; *Driver: Mario Andretti* directed by Richard P. Rubinstein; *Lou Brock/The Thief* directed by Michael Gornick and co-produced with Richard P. Rubinstein; *Pittsburgh's Front Four/The Steel Curtain* directed by Michael Gornick and co-produced with Richard P. Rubinstein; *Rocky Blier/I'm Back* directed by Michael Gornick with Richard P. Rubinstein as co-executive producer; *Terry Bradshaw/Thank God I'm A Country* Boy directed by Michael Gornick with Richard P. Rubinstein as co-executive producer.

1977   Directs, scripts, and edits *Martin*, photographed by Michael Gornick in 16mm color with sepia inserts and blown up to 35mm. Romero's first collaboration with make-up and special effects artist Tom Savini.

1978   Directs, scripts, and co-edits *Dawn of the Dead* (UK title, *Zombies—Dawn of the Dead*), produced by Richard P. Rubinstein. A different version lacking four minutes with re-editing agreed upon by Romero is accomplished by Dario Argento.

1981   Directs, scripts, and co-edits *Knightriders*, produced by Richard P. Rubinstein.

1982   Directs *Creepshow*, produced by Richard P. Rubinstein with screenplay by Stephen King.

1983   Original teleplay "Trick or Treat" for pilot episode of *Tales from the Darkside* included in 1984–85 season, directed by Bob Balaban. Romero is executive producer for this series.

1985   Directs and scripts *Day of the Dead*, produced by Richard P. Rubinstein. Original teleplay "The Devil's Advocate" for 1985–86 season of *Tales from the Darkside* directed by Michael Gornick. Laurel Group partnership dissolves.

1986   Teleplay "Baker's Dozen" adapted from "The Gingerbread Witch" by Scott Edelman for *Tales from the Darkside* directed by John Sutherland. Teleplay "Circus" adapted from a story by Sidney J. Bounds for *Tales from the Darkside* directed by Michael Gornick.

1987   Produces and scripts *Creepshow 2*, directed by Michael Gornick, with stories by Stephen King.

1988   Directs and scripts *Monkey Shines*, produced by Charles Evans.

1990   Directs and scripts "The Facts in the Case of Mr. Valdemar" episode in *Two Evil Eyes*, a two part anthology with Dario Argento, produced by Achille Manzotti for ADC Gruppo Bema Production. Executive producer and scenarist on *Night of the Living Dead* directed by Tom Savini, produced by John A. Russo and Russ Streiner. Released by Twentieth Century Fox as a Menahem Golan production. Scenarist for "The Cat from Hell" episode of *Tales From the Darkside: The Movie*, directed by John Harrison and produced by Richard P. Rubinstein.

1993   Directs, scripts, and executive produced *The Dark Half* based on the novel by Stephen King and produced by Declan Baldwin for Orion Pictures.

2000   Directs and scripts *Bruiser*.

2005   Directs and scripts *Land of the Dead*. Leaves Pittsburgh and moves permanently to Toronto.

2007   Directs and scripts *Diary of the Dead*.

2009   Directs and scripts *Survival of the Dead*.

Filmography

As Director

1968
NIGHT OF THE LIVING DEAD
Almi Films
Director: **George A. Romero**
Producers: Russell Streiner and Karl Hardman
Screenplay: **George A. Romero** and John A. Russo
Cinematography: **George A. Romero**
Editing: **George A. Romero**
Music: Stock Music from the Capitol Hi-Q music library with additional electronic effects by Karl Hardman
Production Company: The Latent Image, Inc. and Hardman Associates, Inc., Pittsburgh
Cast: Duane Jones (Ben), Judith O'Dea (Barbara), Karl Hardman (Harry Cooper), Russell Streiner (Johnny), Marilyn Eastman (Helen Cooper), Keith Wayne (Tom), Judith Ridley (Judy), Kyra Schon (Karen Cooper), Charles Craig (newscaster), Bill Hinzman (cemetery zombie), George Kosana (Sheriff McClelland), Frank Doak (scientist), Bill "Chilly Billy" Cardille (field reporter), Vince Survinski (posse gunman), John A. Russo (zombie in house/military aide in Washington, D.C.), **George A. Romero** (reporter questioning military officials in Washington, D.C.)
96 minutes

1972
THERE'S ALWAYS VANILLA (THE AFFAIR)
Cambist Films
Director: **George A. Romero**
Producers: Russell W. Streiner and John A. Russo
Assistant Producer: Cramer Riblet
Screenplay: Rudolph J. Ricci

Cinematography: **George A. Romero**
Editing: **George A. Romero**
Makeup: Bonnie Priore
Sound: Gary Streiner
Production Manager: Vince Survinski
Music: Rock music performed by Barefoot in Athens with electronic music by Steve Gorn and additional music by Mike Marracino orchestrated by Jim Drake
Production Company: The Latent Image
Cast: Ray Laine (Chris), Judith Streiner (Lynn), Johanna Lawrence (Terri), Richard Ricci (Michael), Roger McGovern (Chris's father)
91 minutes

1973
JACK'S WIFE (HUNGRY WIVES; SEASON OF THE WITCH)
Jack Harris Enterprises
Director: **George A. Romero**
Producer: Nancy M. Romero
Executive Producer: Alvin Croft
Screenplay: **George A. Romero**
Cinematography: **George A. Romero**
Editing: **George A. Romero**
Makeup: Bonnie Priore
Special Effects: Regis Survinski
Production Supervisor: Vince Survinski
Lighting and Additional Photography: Bill Hinzman
Music: Original electronic music by Steve Gorn
Production Company: The Latent Image
Cast: Jan White (Joan), Ray Laine (Gregg), Anne Muffly (Shirley), Jo-edda McClain (Nikki), Bill Thunhurst (Jack), Esther Lapidus (Sylvia), Virginia Greenwald (Marion), Don Mallinger, Dartl Montgomery, Ken Peters, Bob Trow, Bill Hinzman, **George A. Romero** ("ass grabber" at party)
89 minutes

1973
THE CRAZIES (CODE NAME TRIXIE)
Cambist Films
Director: **George A. Romero**
Producer: Alvin Croft

Screenplay: **George A. Romero**, based on an original script by Paul McCollough
Cinematography: Bill Hinzman
Editing: **George A. Romero**
Makeup: Bonnie Priore
Special Effects: Regis Survinski and Tony Pantanello
Production Managers: Bob Rutkowski, H. Cramer Riblett, and Vince Survinski
Sound: Rex Gleason, John Stoll, Eric Baca, and Michael Gornick
Music: Bruce Roberts
Production Company: A Pittsburgh Films Production (through Latent Image)
Cast: Lane Carroll (Judy), W. G. McMillan (David), Harold Wayne Jones (Clank), Lloyd Hollar (Col. Peckham), Lynn Lowry (Kathy), Richard Liberty (Artie), Richard France (Dr. Watts), Harry Spillman (Major Ryder), Will Disney (Dr. Brookmyre), Edith Bell (Lab Technician), W. L. Thunhurst, Jr. (Brubaker), Leland Starkes (Shelby)
103 minutes

1978
MARTIN
Libra Films
Director: **George A. Romero**
Producer: Richard P. Rubinstein
Screenplay: **George A. Romero**
Cinematography: **George A. Romero**
Editing: **George A. Romero**
Special Effects and Makeup: Tom Savini
Sound: Tony Buba
Music: Donald Rubinstein
Production Company: Laurel
Cast: John Amplas (Martin), Lincoln Maazel (Tata Cuda), Christine Forrest (Christina), Elyane Nadeau (Mrs. Santini), Tom Savini (Arthur), Sarah Venable (housewife victim), Fran Middleton (train victim), Al Levitsky (Lewis), **George A. Romero** (Father Howard), James Roy (deacon), Richard Rubinstein (housewife victim's husband)
95 minutes

1979
DAWN OF THE DEAD

United Film Distribution
Director: **George A. Romero**
Producer: Richard P. Rubinstein
Executive Producers: Claudio Argento and Alfredo Cuomo
Screenplay: **George A. Romero**
Cinematography: Michael Gornick
Editing: **George A. Romero**
Script Consultant: Dario Argento
Special Effects and Makeup: Tom Savini
Sound: Tony Buba
Music: The Goblins with Dario Argento; stock library music for American version
Production Company: Laurel
Cast: David Emge (Stephen), Ken Foree (Peter), Scott Reiniger (Roger), Gaylen Ross (Fran), David Crawford (Dr. Foster), David Early (Mr. Berman), Richard France (scientist), Howard Smith (TV commentator), Daniel Dietrich (Givens), Fred Baker (Commander), Jim Baffico (Wooley), Rod Stouffer (young officer on roof), Jese Del Gre (old priest), Clayton McKinnon and John Rice (officers in project apartment), Ted Bank, Patrick McCloseky, Randy Kovitz, and Joe Pilato (officers at police dock), Pasquale Buba, Tony Buba, "Butchie, **George A. Romero** (TV studio director), Christine Forrest (assistant TV studio director)
126 minutes

1981
KNIGHTRIDERS
Laurel
Director: **George A. Romero**
Producer: Richard P. Rubinstein
Executive Producer: Salah M. Hassanein
Screenplay: **George A. Romero**
Cinematography: Michael Gornick
Editing: George A. Romero and Pasquale Buba
Sound: John Butler
Music: Donald Rubinstein
Production Company: Laurel
Cast: Ed Harris (Billy Davis), Gary Lahti (Alan), Tom Savini (Morgan), Amy Ingersol (Linet), Patricia Tallman (Julie), Christine Forrest (Angie), Warner Shook (Pippin), Brother Blue (Merlin), Cynthia Adler (Rockie), John Amplas (Whiteface), Don Berry (Bagman), Amanda Davies

(Sheila), Martin Ferrero (Bontempi), Ken Foree (Little John), Ken Hixon (Steve), John Hostetter (Tuck), Harold Wayne Jones (Bors), Stephen King (hoagie man), Tabitha King (hoagie man's wife)
145 minutes

1982
CREEPSHOW
Warner Bros.
Director: **George A. Romero**
Producer: Richard P. Rubinstein
Executive Producer: Salah M. Hassenein
Screenplay: Stephen King
Cinematography: Michael Gornick
Editing: Pasquale Buba ("The Lonesome Death of Jordy Verrill"), Paul Hirsch ("The Crate"), **George A. Romero** (Prologue, Epilogue, "Something to Tide You Over"), Michael Spolan ("Father's Day", "They're Creeping Up On You")
Special Effects Makeup: Tom Savini
Production Design Special Effects: Cletus Anderson
Production Sound Services: Ledol, Inc.
Music: John Harrison with additional stock library music
Assistant Director: Christine Forrest
First Assistant Director: John Harrison
Production Company: Laurel
Cast: Prologue/Epilogue: Tom Atkins (Billy's father), Iva Jean Saraceni (Billy's mother), Joe King (Billy), Marty Schiff (first garbage man), Tom Savini (second garbage man); "Father's Day": Carrie Nye (Sylvia Grantham), Viveca Lindfors (Aunt Bedelia), Ed Harris (Hank Blaine), Warner Schook (Richard Grantham), Elizabeth Regan (Cass Blaine), Jon Lormer (Nathan Grantham), John Amplas (Dead Nate), Nann Mogg (Mrs. Danvers), Peter Messer (Yarbro); "The Lonesome Death of Jordy Verill": Stephen King (Jordy Verrill), Bingo O'Malley (Jordy's Dad, bank loan officer, Department of Meteors head doctor); "Something to Tide You Over": Leslie Nielsen (Richard Vickers), Ted Danson (Harry Wentworth), Gaylen Ross (Becky Vickers); "The Crate": Hal Holbrook (Henry Northrup), Adrienne Barbeau (Wilma "Billie" Northrup), Fritz Weaver (Dexter Stanley), Robert Harper (Charlie Gereson), Don Keefer (Mike the janitor), Christine Forrest (Tabitha Raymond), Chuck Aber (Richard Raymond), Cletus Anderson (host), Kathie Karlovitz (maid), Darryl Ferruci ("Fluffy"); "They're Creeping Up On You": E. G. Marshall (Upson

Pratt), David Early (White)
122 minutes

1985
DAY OF THE DEAD
United Film Distribution
Director: **George A. Romero**
Producer: Richard P. Rubinstein
Executive Producer: Salah M. Hassanein
Screenplay: **George A. Romero**
Cinematography: Michael Gornick
Editing: Pasquale Buba
Special Makeup Effects: Tom Savini
Art Director: Bruce Miller
Music: John Harrison
Production Company: Laurel
Cast: Lori Cardille (Sarah), Terry Alexander (John), Joseph Pilato (Captain Rhodes), Richard Liberty (Dr. Logan), Howard Sherman (Bub), Jarlath Conroy (McDermott), Antone DiLeo (Miguel), G. Howrd Klar (Steele), Ralph Marrero (Rickles), John Amplas (Fisher), Philip G. Kellams (Torrez), Taso N. Stavrakis (Miller), Gregory Nicotero (Johnson)
102 minutes

1988
MONKEY SHINES
Orion Pictures
Director: **George A. Romero**
Producer: Charles Evans
Screenplay: **George A. Romero**, based on the novel by Michael Stewart
Cinematography: James A. Contner
Editing: Pasquale Buba
Music: David Shire
Production Designer: Cletus Anderson
Cast: Jason Beghe (Allan Mann), John Pankow (Geoffrey Fisher), Kate McNeil (Melanie Parker), Joyce Van Patten (Dorothy Mann), Christine Forrest (Maryanne Hodges), Stephen Root (Dean Burbage)
113 minutes

1990
TWO EVIL EYES
ADC Films
Directors: **George A. Romero** and Dario Argento
Producer: Achille Manzotti
Screenplay: **George A. Romero**, Dario Argento, and Franco Ferrini
"The Facts in the Case of Mr. Valdemar" segment:
Editing: Pasquale Buba
Music: Pino Donaggio
Cast: Adrienne Barbeau (Jessica Valdemar), Ramy Zada (Dr. Robert Hoffman), Bingo O'Malley (Ernest Valdemar) E. G. Marshall (Steven Pike), Tom Atkins (Det. Grogan)
60 minutes

1993
THE DARK HALF
Orion Pictures
Director: **George A. Romero**
Producer: Declan Baldwin
Executive Producer: **George A. Romero**
Screenplay: **George A. Romero**, based on the novel by Stephen King
Cinematography: Tony Pierce Roberts
Editing: Pasquale Buba
Music: Christopher Young
Production Designer: Cletus Anderson
Cast: Timothy Hutton (Thad Beumont/George Stark), Amy Madigan (Liz Beaumont), Julie Harris (Reggie Delesseps), Michael Rooker (Sheriff Alan Pangborn), Robert Joy (Fred Clawson)
122 minutes

2000
BRUISER
Canal+
Director: **George A. Romero**
Executive Producer: Allen M. Shore
Producers: Ben Barenholtz and Peter Grunwald
Screenplay: **George A. Romero**
Cinematography: Adam Swica
Editing: Miune Jan Eramo
Art Direction: Sandra Kybartis

Music: Donald Rubinstein
Cast: Jason Flemyng (Henry Creedlow), Peter Stormare (Milo Styles), Leslie Hope (Rosemary Newley), Nina Garbiras (Janine Creedlow)
99 minutes

2005
LAND OF THE DEAD
Universal Pictures
Executive Producer: Steve Barnett
Producers: Peter Grunwald and Bonnie Goldman
Director: **George A. Romero**
Screenplay: **George A. Romero**
Cinematography: Misoslaw Baszak
Editing: Michael Doherty
Art Direction: Douglas Slater
Music: Reinhold Heil and Johnny Klimak
Cast: Simon Baker (Riley), John Leguizamo (Cholo), Dennis Hopper (Kaufman), Asia Argento (Slack), Robert Joy (Charlie), Eugene Clark (Big Daddy)
97 minutes

2007
DIARY OF THE DEAD
Artfire Films
Executive Producers: Steve Barnett and Donna Croce
Producers: Sam Englebart, Peter Grunwald, Ara Katz, and Art Spiegel
Director: **George A. Romero**
Screenplay: **George A. Romero**
Cinematography: Norman Orenstein
Editing: Adam Swica
Art Direction: John P. Goulding
Music: Norman Orenstein
Cast: Michelle Morgan (Debra Moynihan), Joshua Close (Jason Creed), Shawn Roberts (Tony Ravello), Amy Ciupak Lalonde (Tracy), Joe Dinicol (Eliot Stone), Scott Wentworth (Andrew Maxwell), Alan Van Sprang (Colonel), **George A. Romero** (Police Chief Arthur Katz)
95 minutes

2009
SURVIVAL OF THE DEAD

Artfire Films
Executive Producers: D. J. Carson, Peter Grunwald, Michael Doherty, Ara Katz, and Art Spiegel
Producer: Paula Devonshire
Director: **George A. Romero**
Screenplay: **George A. Romero**
Cinematography: Adam Swica
Editing: Michael Doherty
Art Direction: Joshu de Cartier
Music: Robert Carli
Cast: Alan Van Sprang (Sarge), Kenneth Welsh (Patrick O'Flynn), Kathleen Munroe (Janet/Jane O'Flynn), Devon Bostick (Boy), Richard Fitzpatrick (Seamus Muldoon), Athena Karkanis (Tomboy), Stefano DiMatteo (Francisco), Joris Jarsky (Chuck)
90 minutes

As Screenwriter and Co-Producer Only

1990
NIGHT OF THE LIVING DEAD
Columbia Pictures
Director: Tom Savini
Producers: John A. Russo and Russ Streiner
Executive Producers: Menahem Golan and **George A. Romero**
Screenplay: **George A. Romero**, based on the original screenplay of *Night of the Living Dead* by John A. Russo and **George A. Romero**
Cinematography: Frank Prinzi
Music: Paul McCollough
Production Company: 21st Century Film Corporation
Cast: Tony Todd (Ben), Patricia Tallman (Barbara), Bill Moseley (Johnny)
92 minutes

As Screenwriter Only

1987
CREEPSHOW 2

1990
TALES FROM THE DARKSIDE: THE MOVIE
"Cat from Hell" episode

As Actor Only

1991
THE SILENCE OF THE LAMBS
FBI Chief (uncredited)

2008
DEAD EYES OPEN
Scientist

George A. Romero: Interviews

Night of the Living Dead—
Inter/view with George A. Romero

William Terry Ork and George Abagnalo/1969

Originally published in *INTERVIEW Magazine* 1, no. 4 (1969): 21–22. Courtesy of Inter-view, Inc.

Inter/view: I just saw your film last week and really loved it . . . I had never heard of it until some friend took me to it . . . I understand it was released over a year ago.

Romero: Yes, last October . . . and I've been playing around with it . . . it's been going into distribution overseas and it's being brought back here with *Slaves* . . . that's the package we know about.

Inter/view: It's getting great responses on 42nd Street . . . Is this your first film or have you been doing films for a while?

Romero: I've done mostly commercial things and several experimental things.

Inter/view: Is this all through Latent Image, your company?

Romero: Yes, which has been primarily commercial for the last seven years but we've done a lot of experimentation . . . the group got together by shooting a feature which is still on the shelves . . . we give it a look every once in a while.

Inter/view: Was *Night of the Living Dead* wholly your own production?

Romero: It was entirely ours . . . one of my associates and myself worked on the script and I shot it, directed it, and cut it. We had lots of fun with it and there are parts of it I'm very satisfied with.

Inter/view: Are the people in the rescue squad and the sheriff authentic or are they actors?

Romero: Most are authentic. We had quite a bit of cooperation from people here in the city—police and city fathers. Most of the people were from the small town we shot the scene in and for most of the footage I really didn't have to do much of anything. I ran around with the cameras—I ran about three or four cameras on that—and they were all happy to have guns in their hands. We had quite an arsenal.

Inter/view: They all look intent. Real rednecks.

Romero: The sheriff was particularly good I thought . . . In fact, I gave him a role in a second film we are doing which I should be finished cutting at the end of January.

Inter/view: Are you getting better returns on this new release?

Romero: We have a very good arrangement with Walter Reade. I've heard bad things about them but we can't complain. I'm sure they're taking something somewhere but we are getting more than a fair share.

Inter/view: What was your budget on *Night of the Living Dead*?

Romero: We put $125,000 into it and went completely unencumbered to Reade with $75,000 deferred which brought the final budget to $20,000.* Then on the basis of what *Night of the Living Dead* had done we had no trouble getting the budget for the next picture out of Pittsburgh money sources. We got it from conventional money lenders, in fact, from the banks here, and we went into the second picture with $20,000 in front.

Inter/view: Great! You shot in black in white . . . was that by choice or was color too expensive?

Romero: No, that was by choice. We could have had the budget for color.

Inter/view: In shooting, did you consider composition specifically for black and white?

Romero: Right. I was shooting for that whole kind of flat, somber attitude throughout. I like the look of black and white . . . anyway, I like to photograph in black and white. The film we're working on now is in

* See clarification of NOTLD budget in interviews from 1972, 1973, and 1979.

color and of course most of my photographic experience is in color—commercial stuff—and a lot of it is fun but I really enjoyed working in black and white.

Inter/view: We just read this review in *Reader's Digest* where it warns against taking children to *Night of the Living Dead*. What do you think of this?

Romero: I laughed at the attention that the film received, frankly. When the *Reader's Digest* article appeared it also came out in *Life* and it was editorialized around the country. I was wondering if we could sell on the basis of the way we had the thing cut . . . I wanted to leave the one sequence, the one they called the cannibalism sequence, where the ghouls are having their banquet on the lawn . . . and then Reade picked it up and they wanted some more eating shots and they messed with the cutting a little bit, which disturbed me.

Inter/view: The film has a great integrity to its vision of horror. The ending is really an honest finish to the film and one of absolute nihilism and total hopelessness.

Romero: That was another argument we had . . . It was the topic of weeks of discussion with distributors and it was the basis of a couple of turn downs from New York . . . They thought it was too unmitigated. In fact, when we were producing the film we were taking a risk going all the way to completion without any kind of distribution arrangement. We thought it would be a good property for A.I. but we showed it to them and it was the reason for the turn down there.

Inter/view: They are prudes at the American International. They like fake, cautious horror like Corman's. *Night of the Living Dead* is in the best genre of horror films, especially with the brilliant use of black and white texture and the sense of doom throughout.

Romero: I was dissatisfied with the quality of printing. We have prints that are beautiful that I controlled in the lab here where I normally work.

Inter/view: We will have to come to Pittsburgh to see it.
Romero: You are welcome.

Inter/view: Where did you find Kyra Schon?
Romero: She happens to be really the daughter of the man in the film

who played her father and I thought she had a strange look about her face so I used her.

Inter/view: When the sequence of her eating her father suddenly occurs in silence, the audience shudders.
Romero: I wanted that to be a flat out cut without any further build-up—just to cut to it—and it's a very blatant, ugly shot but I thought it would be effective.

Inter/view: Are you satisfied with Judith O'Dea's performance?
Romero: It was more or less what I could find among actors here and again it was more for a face—it has a very strange quality about it, and I think she is an adequate actress but I wasn't really turned around by her, in fact I cut some things of her out.

Inter/view: There was an incredible tension seeing the people inside the house argue over banal points while the world is coming to an end outside.
Romero: That was the whole thing I went into this film with. I thought once you accept the outlandish premise then just concentrate on the little things that people would get involved in. I didn't want to put any characters like a scientist, just regular people in a farmhouse, and what they would be in disagreement about.

Inter/view: What is your new film about?
Romero: The working title is *At Play with Angels*. It's a film looking at four or five years from now and it's a film looking at quote "the American hippie" four or five years from now and where he is going to be and where the people are going to be around him and what happens to their whole communication.

Inter/view: And it was filmed in Pittsburgh?
Romero: Around Pittsburgh—although we are not using Pittsburgh itself—but a lot of installations on location that are not occupied.

Inter/view: Who do you like in films today?
Romero: Specific films that excited me most last year were *Easy Rider*, *Medium Cool*, and I flipped out over *Putney Swope*.

Inter/view: Oh, your film is much better than any of those . . . What did you do when you were here in New York?

Romero: When I was in school I worked as a grip for studios in New York. I worked out of Columbia's offices, then the small commercial film company here in Pittsburgh, like I said it was virgin country—our commercial operation is going public in 1970 and we hope to open New York offices and we're naturally going to be pursuing the feature thing—that has *always* been my particular goal, of course, and it is with so many people in commercial film. I hope to be able to back into it a lot heavier next year. We have a pending contract right now with a distributor in New York to supply him.

Inter/view: *Night of the Living Dead* should help you.

Romero: I've been very gratified with the reaction. It's doing well everywhere. When it opened in Pittsburgh it broke box office records but we didn't know how much of that was just Pittsburgh because it had a hell of a lot promotion here.

Inter/view: We're depleted with questions. Anything that you would like to say?

Romero: Really the only thing is that I am gratified with the success of the picture and I appreciate your interest and any other message will have to wait until my next film.

Filming *Night of the Living Dead*: An Interview with Director George Romero

Alex Ben Block/1972

From *Filmmakers Newsletter* 5, no.3 (January 1972): 19–24. Reprinted by permission.

Night of the Living Dead is an intentionally crudely made film which its creator feels has been grossly misinterpreted. It is the story of what happens to the eastern United States, and more directly to a group of strangers trapped together in a farmhouse in western Pennsylvania, when a cosmic phenomenon causes the dead to return to life.

In the opening scene blonde Barbara and her brother Johnny are attacked, without provocation, by a zombie-like middle-aged man in a torn, rumpled suit. Johnny is killed and Barbara, near hysteria, flees to a nearby farmhouse.

After a few anxious moments Barbara is joined by Ben, the strong black lead, who sets to boarding up doors and windows to fend off the growing horde of macabre-looking characters whose number seems to be constantly growing.

While dashing about madly looking for barricades Ben reveals the problem to Barbara who is slowly withdrawing into shock. Because of a freak molecular mutation due to the ill-gotten return of a space probe, the dead are rising and devouring the living.

While the theater audience wonders whether to laugh or scream Ben and Barbara discover they are not alone in the farmhouse. Judy and Tom, a teenage couple, and Helen, Harry, and their daughter Karen have been hiding in the basement.

Ben and Harry argue. Barbara becomes a vegetable. Judy and Tom act brave and scared. Helen nurses Karen who has been bitten by one of the Living Dead.

A radio is made to work and an announcer proceeds to explain the mass dimensions of the problem—something we are constantly re-

8

minded of by flashes of the ballooning legion of reignited corpses ever pounding on the farmhouse door. As the attackers grow stronger, internal dissension makes the tiny band in the farmhouse weaker. Tom and Judy try to escape, fail, and become the ghouls' lunch.

With a posse of vigilantes and police on the way Ben accidentally shoots Harry. Barbara is eaten by her brother who has become a ghoul. Helen discovers little Karen in the basement eating Harry's arm, and is then killed herself by her own daughter. Only Ben, now hiding in the basement, is still alive when dawn and the posse arrive.

But the ending is not happy, and it is this, perhaps, more than any other factor in the film which has caused critics to call the film "the standard to which all subsequent horror films will be compared."

The area around where the Monongahela and Allegheny Rivers meet to form the Ohio, in downtown Pittsburgh, is known as the Golden Triangle. Headquartered within its radius are U.S. Steel, Gulf Oil, Westinghouse, Alcoa, and The Latent Image. This latter corporation is known for its productions of *The Calgon Story, Ketchup, Heinz Pickle No. 1,* and *Night of the Living Dead.*

Newsday called *NOTLD* ". . . the best horror movie ever made." It "spooked the living daylights out of" Rex Reed. *Newsweek* described it as "a true horror classic . . ." It was created on an initial investment of $6,000 out of the frustration of a group of under-thirty filmmakers who couldn't finance the feature they really wanted to make, and it has already grossed over $3 million.

What follows is an edited interview with George Romero done on a recent winter morning in his small yellow office with the lion's head stapler on the cluttered desk and various clippings and promotion pieces for Latent Image projects on one corkboard wall. The office outside is noisy with film-related activities. The hall walls are lined with awards from the advertising industry for outstanding commercials. George Romero is relaxed and in full command.

AB: Would you describe the development of *Night of the Living Dead* from the beginning?
GR: We had $6,000 and a loose idea based on a short story I'd written which was in fact an allegorical thing. We decided to take that and turn it into a real blood and guts film, and that's how it started.

The six originally in our group came from different fields. One was an attorney because we needed to incorporate. Two of the people were from a recording studio in town because at that time we didn't have our own as we now do downstairs. One of the investors later on was a butcher, and that's where we got the intestines. He brought them out to the set and we said, "That's great."

A friend and I began writing a script, but we didn't have it nearly completed when we started shooting. We cast around for people. That as kind of a random experience too: there wasn't much to draw on in Pittsburgh except a friend of ours, Duane Jones, who is the black actor who plays Ben in the picture. We had no preconceived notion as to the role being a black role, Duane came in, he looked right, he read well, so we used him. We never took any further note of it. It's not mentioned in the script at all, although I know we're getting a lot of press comment over that fact. Somebody, I forget who, mentioned that when he dies you can hear the strain of "Old Man River" on the soundtrack, but it's just not there at all.

The blond girl, Barbara, is a Pittsburgh girl who was on the West Coast and happened to come back into town about then, so we used her. And the younger girl was a secretary here and her boyfriend was a guy who was doing nightclub gigs so we used him too. Harry Cooper and his wife were the two investors from the recording studio, and their little girl is Harry's girl in real life. So that was the group.

Then for the ghouls: whenever we needed people, we just recruited people. It was mostly our clients and friends. We just said, "C'mon out, we'll have a ball." And we always had kegs of beer and a lot of food and got as many as we needed every time [chuckles remembering]. We wound up paying them all S.A.G. wages as the money came in later, but nobody was paid on the spot. No one knew whether the film would be distributed or what; but once we started we had to keep rolling because we had commercials to shoot, so we started before everything was complete.

We shot in several lumps of time, and I had an idea where we were going with the thing. I had in the back of my mind the whole time the old DC comic books—you know, *Tales of the Crypt* and stuff like that. I used to be a big comic fan, although I don't think I am now except maybe in a nostalgic way. Most of the lines were written, some the night before. We'd sit around knowing the direction the thing had to go and write dialogue. Some of it, out of frustration, we just went flat out with, doing the obvious like, "We may not enjoy living together, but dying together won't solve anything."

The story was an allegory written to draw a parallel between what people are becoming and the idea that people are operating on many levels of insanity that are only clear to themselves. But we didn't really try to write that stuff in and we didn't shoot it for the pat explanations or anything. We shot it just the way things would be if the dead returned to life. For instance, we let the news commentator write his own copy. We gave him the germ of the idea and he was a newsman and wrote his copy; and the sheriff and the posse, we didn't try to gloss them up at all—we just shot a bunch of people. We gave them guns and they kind of just went ahead. The sheriff wasn't actually a sheriff or an actor. He was just a mill hand. Just a beautiful guy. One of those guys you can put in front of a camera or in front of ten thousand people and he'll just be himself.

AB: What equipment did you use?
GR: We shot entirely in 35mm. We used two Arriflex thirty-fives, one in a blimp. We used all quartz lights. It was all the stuff we had. We used one Nagra for sound, with one microphone, although we used lavalieres in a couple of sequences. Although we used two cameras we never had both rolling simultaneously on any of the sync sound footage. We had the blimp housing for one camera, and all the sound is the location sound. We didn't dub anything, except for one or two words during the escape sequence because we were shooting wild. But the rest of it was the actual sound in the house, and in most cases you can hear it. I mean, it has kind of a hollow sound, but I thought it was pretty successful for being purely location stuff, and some of it was pretty difficult to stage.

The make-up was done by Harry and Helen Cooper, the people that played Harry and Helen in the film, that is. We didn't really need very much. None of the effects make-up was very heavy. For costuming we just went around and picked things out—old clothes lying in people's attics, etc.

AB: What stock did you use to achieve your purposes?
GR: It was all 35mm negative. Plus X mostly. Four X in some of the night stuff. Tri X where we wanted to create some grain, even when we were inside the house. We wanted that flat kind of graininess when Barbara first enters the house and when Ben first arrives and is rummaging around looking for supplies and so forth. We wanted to create a depressing or oppressing air to the thing.

AB: Was your use of black and white intentional?

GR: No, budgetary. If we'd gone to color it would have been part of the strategy of walking the line again, because it's very difficult to get a black and white picture distributed. We had a hell of a time because we were in black and white. In fact, there were quite a few arguments about it. When you talk to distributors the main criteria they use in determining a film's worth has nothing at all to do with the picture itself. It's all of the formula things, and it's amazingly frustrating.

AB: What was your shooting ratio on . . . *Dead*? What ratio do you like to work on?

GR: I'd like to work infinity to one [laughs]. I overshoot. When I shoot something I'm directing I shoot everything. Because we had such little seed money, though, on *Living Dead*, I think we came in at twelve to one. And I was amazed. I was saying until the last day, we're not going to make it.

AB: What do you consider a realistic ratio?

GR: For the way I produce I like to budget a film at thirty-five or forty to one, which may sound high, but we wind up shooting it. It's a luxury I know, but we shot *Vanilla* in 16mm and *Jack's Wife* in 16mm, and shooting 16 I was able to spill the stuff out of the camera and I just loved it.

AB: How long were you actually in production?

GR: It took about a seven-month period, but there were only thirty production days in there because we shot for two weeks and then we broke, then we shot again for a few days, and then we broke again. As I said, we were shooting around a commercial schedule we had to keep which really made it a bitch.

AB: Didn't that make continuity difficult?

GR: Yes, but we really didn't have any alternative. And really, it's not like we were trying to maintain any kind of subtle mood. The attitude of that film can be understood in an instant; and you just kind of get yourself into that attitude and go out and do it.

AB: What were some of your problems as director?

GR: Primarily to forget that we were making a horror film. I just wanted them to appear as though they were worried about a snowstorm or something. I didn't want anybody to get very intense with it except in the areas where we just threw up our hands and went camp with it and then we just had fun. In some sequences I just wanted them to move and say lines rather unobtrusively. Just get through it comfortably. A lot of the time I'd create the situation and get them moving before I'd even pick up the camera. Like in the sieges and some of the bigger scenes, I'd just get the situation going and walk around and look at it for awhile, then I'd pick up the camera and start shooting.

AB: What was the most difficult scene to do?
GR: I guess the escape sequence out of the farmhouse. There was the gun shooting, and fire, and explosions which never really came off all that well. That was the most difficult scene logistically and as far as special effects go. And it was all night stuff.

AB: Was it something you could shoot only once?
GR: We had two trucks we'd bought for $35 apiece and they ran, so we had another shot if we screwed up, but we got it the first time. That scene was shot wild. We took the other Arri out of the blimp and used both wild.

AB: How'd you get the police cooperation?
GR: We just called them up and said, "We're shooting a film," and they said, "Oh yeah." And we said, "Yeah, this is what we need. We need police cars, wagons, men, dogs, weapons." The policemen in uniform were real, and a lot not in uniform were off-duty cops that came and brought weapons and things. No problems at all. We weren't shooting in the city, so we didn't have to get involved with permits; but we found it very easy to get cooperation.

We just scrounged everything else we needed. The farmhouse was on a deserted farm that was going to be ripped down and we went out and rented it for the summer. We just convinced them not to rip it down until the summer was over.

AB: You also did editing (as well as being cameraman and director). Was that phase difficult?
GR: It was from the standpoint that when I direct I don't think of the cutting, I'll go out and shoot a sequence like those sieges at the house and I'll literally wait until I see something I want to shoot. I don't log it or do anything with it. I just go back and look at the footage and get

familiar with it, then decide how I want to cut it. And I'm often left short that way.

AB: Rex Reed calls *Living Dead* "crudely made." Does that bother you?
GR: No. I agree with him. Some of it's intentional. In other words, some of the graininess and some of the simplicity is intentional. We make a living making a glass of beer look like heaven, and we could have glossed this up too. This is one of the talents our shop has, making things look beautiful. Maybe that's why we went as far the other way as we did. We used as often as possible what was there. We tried to be as unpretentious as possible in designing the sets. And we were. The house was bare. There was thought behind everything we brought into that farmhouse.

AB: *Newsweek* called *Dead* "a step beyond in gore." Was this intentional?
GR: It was to the extent that we felt that films aren't usually made this graphic. But why not? You know what's happening. Why cut away when you know exactly what's going on? We got the intestines, and we showed the ghouls going at them, and we said, "Well, we're just going to leave that stuff in" [spoken like a defiant little boy imitating a vampire].

AB: Do you feel your personality comes through in the film?
GR: No. [big laugh] Well, it does in some of the sequences—in the ones I could shoot the way I enjoy shooting, primarily the action sequences where I could get really involved. Cinematically I think that's the only place you can see my style, if I have a style.

AB: Do you have a style?
GR: I think so. I enjoy doing jigsaw puzzles. I like to shoot and cut my own material. If I had to define my style I'd say it was almost cubist. Like if I had to shoot what was happening in this room right now I'd just be all over the place and not making any decisions at all until I had the material. I'd cut it so I could look at the film and remember exactly what was happening from many different points of view. It would be cubist. It other words, there wouldn't necessarily be any relation between shot to shot, but my cutaways would be informational cutaways. They'd be quick and I'd cut down as much as I could to go for as many angles and viewpoints as I could.

AB: Two of your three films have dealt with the occult. Are you a student of the black arts?

GR: No. [laughs]

AB: How did you finance the film?

GR: We financed the film as we went along. We formed a separate corporation to shoot it and we were stealing a bit from the Latent Image kitty to keep the thing rolling. We got enough to put a couple sequences in the can, cut it, and then showed it to people. At that time we started to sell stock at two different levels. I forget what the exact structure was. Then when we got it down to a final interlock and needed all of our money to finish it and print it, we sold stock at a higher price. All in all it was a small amount involved. $70,000 was the cash we had in when we finally put it in the distributor's hands, and $114,000 was the money after the deferments to the actors were paid off.

AB: How did you go about approaching distributors?

GR: We told the distributors that this film had some potential beyond just an ordinary "blood-and-guts" piece. No one, of, course, listened to that. It was our first time out of the gate. We didn't have final cut approvals; we didn't have anything, when we finally signed with the Walter Reade Organization. They gave it good promotion, but a flat, drive-in blood-and-guts promotion.

The film did pretty well when it first came out. Immediately we had indications that it was unique. It started to get editorialized by *Readers Digest*, *Life Magazine*, and people were saying, "This is about the grossest thing possible. How far will you go to make money?"

AB: Can you name some specific things you think a distributor looks for?

GR: OK. For example, color. Identifiable talents. Identifiable musical talents if there aren't any on screen. Pace. Action. And I don't mean "here's a scene with the pacing wrong." I don't mean anything that might be valid. I'm talking about real, you know, "Well, it needs some action here. I don't care what it is." It's like you walk into a distributor's office and see that chart on his wall where he knows in May of '72 he's got to release a Sean Connery piece, and he doesn't give a damn what it is, except in that particular time, in order to advance Connery and to advance the studio, they have to release something there. And beyond that nothing matters. And that really is true, and it's a very frustrating experience.

We went to four or five distributors before going with Reade. Columbia showed a great deal of interest. In fact, they told us their main reason for turning it down was that it was in black and white. And AIP then said it was too unmitigated. They said, "Well, if you shoot a happy ending to the thing, or shoot the guy surviving, or develop a romantic interest, then maybe we'll talk about it."

AB: Is Hollywood dead?

GR: Hollywood is dead, but the distributor ain't! Hollywood has moved is all that's happened. I'll be happy when there is finally a coalition of producers that are distributing because you cannot get the most basic filmic understanding from any one commercial distributor. You have people who've been attorneys. You have people who've been in other cut-throat businesses and who are looking at it from a purely business point of view. They all think they [snapping fingers] can call the shot as to what's gonna really sell this season—and none of them really know. They analyze the most basic aspect of the last film that was a big hit, and they think they can duplicate that and they don't. There isn't going to be the same kind of trend each season. A good film's going to make it, and for several reasons: Maybe it'll be that the film has a certain attitude or a certain viewpoint that hasn't been adopted before; or maybe it'll even be the topical, exploitable content of the film that makes it successful. But that's not all there is to it.

AB: What else is there?

GR: I put, maybe jadedly, a heavy weight on the promotion, although again, it's a combination of reasons. But I think a film is largely sold to the public. I don't think *Easy Rider* would have done anything at all (it might have been a *Living Dead* kind of thing) had it not had the promotion that it had.

AB: Would you like to work on a commercially backed production?

GR: Maybe. It's just because I don't have the experience, but I would want it to be a certain way and I don't know if I could get that. I just don't know. I don't know that power, and again, I'm very suspicious because of the corporate involvement we've had. I don't know what the pecking order is, I don't know who really pulls those strings. I don't know what happens over in that machine. I don't know when you get involved in a production like, say, *Rosemary's Baby*, how much does Polanski really do? Or how much does the art director do? Or how much does Mia Farrow do? Or how much does Mia Farrow's agent do? I just don't know. I've been so involved with the hassling and back-stabbing at the level *we're* operating under, that I wonder what it might be like when you're talking about *that* kind of money and to *that* many people who are either stars or have the power; and I just don't know what it's like; but I'm very afraid of it. I really am.

I feel this whole phase these past three years has been very temporary. I don't know where I'm going to be two years from now, and it's almost like OK. I've jumped into the corporate hassle right now, and I'm swimming blind to get through with this phase of it, hoping after each project that we get a distributor or take a step towards solvency and that maybe it'll be the last step.

If I haven't achieved, under this structure, the kind of solvency and creative freedom that's going to allow me to stay with it, I don't know what I'll do. I might go with a commercial shop exclusively, go purely for the bread. I don't really think I'd want to go into the studio thing. I think I'd rather be a commercial director because I think you're really more flexible. I don't trust the studio system. I don't know what it'd be like, but I know the commercial market pretty well; and I know I can exist in it with very little being sand-papered off of me.

My primary thing is wanting to be in control. The only reason I've enjoyed being with this company is that I've been the president of it since it's existed. The main thing I've gotten out of it is being able, in every aspect, to do exactly what I've wanted to do.

The one thing I hope any recognition I receive brings is just this. When I walk in, I will be able to say: "This is the way it's going to be done." And that's the way I would hope it will be.

Romero: An Interview with the Director of *Night of the Living Dead*

Sam Nicotero/1973

From *Cinefantastique* 2, no. 3 (Winter 1973): 8–15. Reprinted by permission.

When Continental Films dumped *Night of the Living Dead* onto the summer/fall drive-in circuit in 1968 with a typically gross exploitation campaign, who could have expected that this cheap, black and white horror film was anything more than what it appeared to be? Indeed, Continental Films and the entire distribution system has since been subject to criticism, that a film of undeniable merit such as George Romero's *Night of the Living Dead* was thrown away on the exploitation circuit like so many other trashy films. But really, even if Continental had realized the merit of the film that had come into their hands, would anyone have believed them if they had tried to market it on that basis? Probably not, because *Night of the Living Dead* is a cheap, black and white horror film and it is beyond public acceptance that it can also be a brilliant work of cinematic art.

Director George Romero is one of the film's makers that is chiefly responsible for its unexpected intelligence and sophistication. *Night of the Living Dead* was the collaborative effort of two Pittsburgh commercial film companies, The Latent Image, Inc., George Romero's company, and Hardman Associates, Inc., the firm of Karl Hardman who produced *Night of the Living Dead* with Russell W. Streiner. Both firms are still active at present in the production of advertising and promotional films, which is their primary business. The filming of *Night of the Living Dead* was completed over a number of months, during weekends and evenings, and during periods between regular film assignments. The company was shorthanded and attracted actors and technicians on a deferred payment basis, with most everyone participating for the fun of it or for the experience. The producers themselves doubled up with acting roles, Karl Hardman appearing as the ruthless coward Harry, and Russell Streiner as Johnny, the first victim of the ghouls in the film's opening scene. George Romero worked as his own cinematographer and also edited the film, and members of producer Streiner's family were pressed into service, Gary Streiner working as sound engineer and Jaqueline Streiner handling the script coordination and continuity.

George Romero has since gone on to produce three other films under the auspices of his Latent Image company, with distribution to be handled by Cambist Films: *There's Always Vanillia* (retitled *The Affair*), a sentimental romantic drama, *Jack's Wife*, a story of witchcraft and the supernatural in suburbia, and *The Crazies*, dealing with the accidental contamination of a New England town with the weapons of biological warfare.

CFQ: Do you have any special interest or fondness for making "horror films"?

Romero: I didn't in the beginning. When we made *Night of the Living Dead*, we made it as our first picture and our friends in distribution circles told us to make something exploitive because it's safer. So we decided to do a "horror film." Now when we did it, we said, we're not just going to do a horror film, we're going to really "go out" with it and try and make it "gutsy."

So then I got into that. I got into a fascination with it from the standpoint that it hasn't really been done very often. I have a theory that there are so many films that haven't been done, that *have* been done a hundred times, but haven't been done yet.

One of them for example, like one of the films that I really want to do and I'm talking to some people about it now, is *Tarzan of the Apes*. Because it hasn't been done yet. I'd like to do it exactly the way Burroughs wrote it, and I think it would be a tremendous piece of Victorian kind of escapism. There's an example of it. There's been what, twenty-five or thirty Tarzan films made and it's never been made that way.

We've been digressing a little bit, but that's how I got into *Night of the Living Dead*, and since then I've had kind of a fascination with the macabre. Coming off *Living Dead* I got into kind of a study of the occult. Our third film, *Jack's Wife*, is an occult film. Which I think, again, takes a little bit of a different approach to the study, not so much of the occult, but how it works on somebody's mind. Of course, that's been done, but we kind of combined it with contemporary life and what's going on today. We took a suburban housewife with all her frustrations, and all of the women's lib being pumped into her, and did it from the standpoint of this woman whose head gets all messed up with it without any real understanding. The film doesn't claim that there's any efficacy in magic, witchcraft, anything like that, it's just purely in her head. It's not a metaphysical film really. It's a film about what happens to this woman who doesn't know what she's fooling around with, but starts fooling around with it and then starts wondering what she's doing and wondering whether it's working.

CFQ: To get it straight, for the record, you have four films to your credit. Is that right?
Romero: I'm cutting, now, the fourth film, which is *The Crazies*, the one you're in.

CFQ: Do you feel *The Crazies* is your best?
Romero: Well, so far, technically, I think it's the best. I think in certain aspects of it I was more successful in getting what I wanted. Of course this is the first time that I've had enough of a budget and enough people and enough sets, you know, exactly what I needed. So I think from that standpoint it's the most successful one, although I think *Jack's Wife* is probably a better film . . .

CFQ: . . . than *Living Dead*?
Romero: No, than *The Crazies* . . . but I don't think it will do as well at the box office.

CFQ: Are there any horror films that have influenced you, do you feel?
Romero: Influenced me? I don't know.

CFQ: Your shadows, I see a lot of shadows in your work, which I think is good . . .
Romero: I don't know. That might be influenced more by my background and training as a painting and design student, I think. I just have a concentration on composition and lighting and aspects like that.

CFQ: Were you born in New York City?
Romero: Yea.

CFQ: How long have you been based in Pittsburgh?

Romero: I came out here to go to school, came out here to go to Carnegie Tech and study painting and design and Spanish background. I'm, I guess maybe, influenced a little by the Spanish painters. I think that perhaps my approach to the visualization of something comes out of that rather than any influence from any director or cinematographer that I've studied.

CFQ: I think that may be what gives a film that Romero touch.

Romero: I think that anyone who has an eye for composition, or anyone who has an eye for a translation of anything to a two-dimensional format is influenced by two-dimensional things that he's seen, not so much by film. You can't really study a film. No matter how many times you watch a film, you may see any given shot for a matter of, in the aggregate, two or three minutes, whereas you can look at a painting or a graphic or a painting that you have in your home or something that you really like, endlessly. You may stare at a painting for hours.

CFQ: The theme of the first film that you did, *Night of the Living Dead*, how did you develop it?

Romero: Well, I wrote a short story which dealt with, which was in fact, an allegory, a statement about society, which dealt with a siege by the living dead. It was much less contrived, I think, than the film is, from the standpoint that it was purely allegorical. Now a lot of the people that have seen the film are seeing the allegory coming out of the film anyway.

CFQ: I've heard it called a political film.

Romero: That, maybe, was in my head when directing it, when we were looking for an approach to it, but I don't think it is really reflected. I wasn't actually thinking of it, wasn't conscious of it, with the exception of a few scenes, like the scenes with the posse and of course the final scene. It wasn't a conscious effort on my part to direct that allegory into the film, but I guess it was a strong enough influence that it came out anyway and people are seeing it's there.

CFQ: Did you have any trouble with the cast and crew, getting them to take it seriously, because it was a horror film?

Romero: Not really, no. Course, we've always had a pretty good group of people. We have a totally in-house unit. We work with each other well. We know what our intentions are and we don't have any internal strife or anything like that so we have a pretty good time. You have fun no matter what you're doing. You can be doing *Hamlet* and I think you'll have fun doing it.

CFQ: In horror cinema there are two techniques, the suggestive school, which creates a feeling of horror indirectly through the viewer's imagination, and the graphic school, which visually shocks the viewer. You seem to do both pretty well. Could you discuss your technique and approach in this context?

Romero: Well I prefer the subtler approach, really, which wouldn't be indicated by *Night of the Living Dead*, which is why I think I am happier with *Jack's Wife* than I am with *Living Dead* or with *The Crazies*. I'm into Don Siegel pretty hard. *Invasion of the Body Snatchers* was a tremendous film which had a little bit of both, but it was more suggestive. It was more moody. The horror was more subtle.

CFQ: The actual production of *Night of the Living Dead*, did you have any trouble getting money or backing for it?

Romero: Yea. It was our first time out and Pittsburgh is a very wealthy city, but it's the kind of money that's in Pittsburgh; it's not gambling money; it's nuts and bolts industrial money. It's very difficult. When we first went around, we tried for about three years before we made *Living Dead* to get people to fund some kind of a project, thinking all along that we were going to do a serious piece. In fact, we had a script written, that I had written, that we were trying to promote. We had an entire package put together and we couldn't get any cash here and we tried to get cash out of New York. People were interested in the script, but they wanted to buy it, take it away, and make it. We said no, our idea is to make the film. When we told people here that we're going to make a feature film that's going to be released they would say: "Uh huh, oh yea," and walk away from you. That was that. We just couldn't do it. We finally formed another corporation. There were ten of us, and the corporation was called Image Ten. That's where it got its name. We each put in a little bit of seed money, which was enough to buy our film stock, and we talked to the cast on the basis of deferred payments. The cast agreed and we started to shoot and of course we had, and we still do, commercial and industrial films. And so that film was shot over a period, with great breaks, over a period of about nine months, with great breaks in between to come back and do a pickle commercial or something, which was distressing. After we got some footage in the can where we could screen rushes for people, people started coming 'round saying: "Hey, that looks like a movie!" and we said, well that's what it is! And they said: "Oh yea," and they started to put up money and of course then we sold stock in the corporation which we already had formed and got the whole thing complete so that we had it completely funded when we went into New York, unencumbered. In other words, we didn't have any outstanding debts to any labs or anything like that which we were anticipating, so that was lucky for us in that we didn't have to give up any percentages to get it finished, and we have yet to have to do that.

CFQ: Who is John A. Russo?
Romero: He wrote the script with me. We actually collaborated on it. It was based on a story that I wrote and when I started to mete it out towards a screenplay we had to start shooting film, because we figured we were going to have interruptions and we were running out of weather. I had written about half of it and at that point turned it over to Jack and he and I worked on the rest of it. He would do drafts on it and come up to the location and we'd work it out.

CFQ: Did you work from a complete script from the beginning, or work it out as you went?
Romero: We had the structure, we had the scenario, but we did some of the scenes—in fact I can remember one morning sitting out on the porch of that house and writing a scene that we shot that afternoon because we happened to have the people together.

CFQ: What particular scene was that?
Romero: It was the little interchange. It's a difficult scene for anyone to remember that isn't really into the film. It's a little scene where Helen Cooper comes up from the cellar and says: "There's another broadcast at three ayem," or something, "Maybe we should try to make it to the car." And Ben, Duane Jones, is saying: "You have a car?" It's where Ben discovers that they have a car, when he wants to know where it is.

CFQ: Was there anything cut from the final version of *Night of the Living Dead* that you would have preferred to have left in? And if you could change it now, what would you do?
Romero: Yea, there were a few things. The feast on the front lawn was

inserted again where I had another cut, towards the end of the film when they're watching the second telecast they look out the window and I had expansive shots of the fields with just the ghouls dotting the countryside, which I felt at that point would have been more effective, but the distributor insisted that we cut back to the ghouls eating flesh. I said, no, we've had that, but of course, I didn't get my way.

The film was about ten minutes longer. That was a couple of more dialogue scenes that I felt were kind of important that help set up the characterizations of some of the people, background stuff on the people.

CFQ: This seems to happen to almost every film nowadays.

Romero: It depends on who you are. That was our first one out, and of course, even on this last one, *The Crazies*, we had distributor interference. The first three films we did on spec, from the standpoint that we got the funding, we took the risks, we signed the notes for the money and we went in without having discussed the film with the distributor other than very superficially with regard to, what do you think about this script, or, are we gonna sit with this on the shelf. In some cases, in the case of *There's Always Vanilla* we went ahead despite urgings from the distributors to not bother to make it. We went ahead and made it and it is now in distribution. We have not been hurt too badly by it.

CFQ: Besides making a lot of money, *Night of the Living Dead* had pretty good critical reviews from a lot of people. Did you expect that, that it would get the accolades that it did?

Romero: No. I knew some people were going to like it. I knew what it had, I knew that it had some guts and I knew that certain things in it were cinematically successful. I really didn't think that people would see that allegory. Maybe I was underestimating. I don't think most people do see it, because it is very subtle. Often times I laugh about some of the interpretations read into it. We've had some outlandish things said about it. I know that aspects of it are cinematically successful. I didn't expect this much critical acclaim, which has really bowled me over, and it seems to be universal. We get press from overseas and it's the same old story. We get better press out of the city. Our press in Pittsburgh isn't very good, but we're getting tremendous press everywhere else.

I didn't expect that much because there are so many things in the film that I consider to be bad. There's so much terrible dialogue and there are several really poor performances. Technically, the film is not that bad, but Christ, our commercial work is better than that! We were working under such adverse conditions. And I think being so close to the project from those standpoints I felt that those were too glaring to be overlooked.

CFQ: Do you think the *Reader's Digest* article helped the film, or hindered it?

Romero: That kind of stuff never hurts. People that write biting things like that are defeating their own purpose because all they do is create a lot of curiosity. That might not be entirely true. There might be some parents who read that and then didn't send their kids to see it, which is just as well. That was picked up from a newspaper article and was then picked up by *Life* magazine, and was quoted by *Life* magazine. The film had some controversy right from the jump. But the film really didn't have its big life in its first release. It went out as a showcase piece. It went out with a film called *Dr. Who and the Daleks*, which was an English thing. It circulated around and made good money and it did get some damn good word of mouth. It was on the "drive-in circuit" and it was because it was so gutsy and unmitigated and unrelenting.

CFQ: Was it only financial considerations that forced you to do *Night of the Living Dead* in black and white? Would you do it in color now? What do you think of color horror films as compared to black and white?

Romero: I think you can do a good job. You have to be very careful with color. Not as much now as you used to with the development of the new stocks and so forth. You can get good, subtle stuff. I think a lot of people were afraid of color for a long time because you had to light it brilliantly, you had that pop-in Technicolor look. You can do subtle things with color now and that's purely a technical development, so I'm not afraid of color. I don't know what I would have done had the money been available. The decision to do it in black and white was budgetary, in answer to that question which everyone asks. But I don't know really, it's a question I can't answer. I couldn't answer that question unless I knew that I had the money for color and actively chose black and white and then I could say, yea, I actively did it. I don't know. Right now, I feel that it's better in black and white and I don't know if I'd have gone with color or not. I really don't.

CFQ: Do you feel that comedy is appropriate in horror films?
Romero: Oh sure.

CFQ: Or do you feel it is counterproductive? Hammer Films very sel-
dom have humor. Does it make it almost camp when it's too serious?
Romero: I think it does. Hammer films have excellent production
values, they have a tremendous feel for that gothic aura, they have
good people, they have good actors, substantial people, but there is
something about their films that are just . . . you know . . . stiff upper
lip, and every damn one is exactly the same. There's something about
it that's just, you know, it's kind of on a line and you never get off it. I
think you can go one way or another with it, and I don't think it has a
counterproductive value at all.

There's stuff in *Living Dead* that gets a kind of nervous laughter. Well,
we saw this twenty-five minutes of *The Crazies* here, and there's a few
laughs in it, but they're kind of nervous laughs, they're a release. I
know Hitchcock has a philosophy, he will always follow a very tense
sequence with a little piece of comedy. He does it all the time. If you
study his work, it works very well. In *Living Dead* we have a couple of
instances like that. Right in the middle of the uptight-thing with the
posse, the sheriff, what he is saying is straight, in fact that was an ad
lib interview, I left some of the things in purely for the chuckle. I don't
think that it's counterproductive at all.

CFQ: Does it bother you when you're in an audience, say with your
own film, and the audience reacts differently than you expected them
to. Does it bother you at all?
Romero: No. I always find it interesting. I really think than anyone
that endeavors to do anything creative is really trying to communicate,
and reaching people in any way is a substantial thing.

When I was acting I did a play called *The Connection*, and played a
character named Leach, and I had to come down center stage and take
a needle in the arm, and take an overdose and wind up going into fits
and wind up with my arm hanging off the proscenium with the needle
hanging out of the vein. We did it with nose putty. And every night
it was a different reaction. It was really a tremendous thing. We got
nervous laughter to that, we got some cringing, we got some people in
nausea, and it's just that you know that you're doing something. That's
a gratifying thing. I think I've seen *Night of the Living Dead* with audi-

ences three or four times, other than in private screenings with smaller groups. It has, pretty much, a uniform reaction.

CFQ: I've got the stock "Johnny Carson" question coming up. Sex and nudity has become increasingly evident in recent horror films. Do you regard this obligatory nudity as an obstacle or a nuisance?

Romero: I think it's a nuisance from the standpoint that I don't know how much of my life I've spent arguing with distributors over how much and how little and so forth. It gets a little bit ludicrous when you're sitting around saying thirty-six frames of tit rather than twenty-four. I don't understand it. I think if you want to use it, and it serves a purpose then you should use it.

CFQ: You're almost a pioneer, in that *Night of the Living Dead* features one of the first bare asses seen in horror films!

Romero: (laughter) I don't think so. No.

CFQ: At the time of that film you didn't have all the ratings and all the nudity in films.

Romero: No. In fact it was just on the cusp. The rating system was just coming in. That film wasn't rated.

CFQ: What do you think *The Crazies* should get? I don't think it should get an R.

Romero: I don't think it should get an R, but I think it will. In the first place, an independent has a hell of a harder time with the people that decide the ratings than a major studio does. Actually, I don't think the rating system makes any sense, frankly. I think all the X rating did was license a lot of meaningless pornography. I think that a sexual passage in a film, if it's gonna mean something, is fine, and I don't give a damn how graphic it is. I don't have any compunctions about shooting one, if it has its place, but I won't do it randomly. In fact, I had arguments all over hell on *Jack's Wife* with the distributors. There are two sexual passages in *Jack's Wife*, and I had all kinds of hell telling people "no," it makes no sense to make these porno, because it's just gonna detract. The woman wants and needs sexual release and the first one is the most graphic of the two because she finally gets it after forty-five minutes of ponderous film. You need enough to show that release. To show the change in her. But you didn't have to go that graphic with it.

Living Dead got an X rating in Great Britain because they take violence into account as much or more than morality when rating their product over there and I do think that that makes some sense. I don't know that any of that stuff does any damage to a developing mind watching it. I don't know that any kid, unless he's disturbed to begin with, is going to see something happening on the screen and go out and immediately do it. I don't think any kid is gonna go and watch *A Clockwork Orange* and go out and find a rubber phallus and go out and start beating somebody with it. I might be wrong. I may do some harm. I really don't think so. I do think that possibly violence is gonna affect people more than seeing sex on the screen. I don't think that pornography is unhealthy really, in that sense. It might be very healthy.

CFQ: Duane Jones is the only character in *Night of the Living Dead* about whom we are given no information about background, job, family, or residence, and as he is the central character, why was this done?
Romero: One of the scenes I mentioned earlier that was cut, was one of the background scenes. It gave a little bit of his background and told who he was and where he was going.

CFQ: What has Duane Jones done since *Night of the Living Dead*?
Romero: He's always been active. He's acting. He's in New York City. He's done some off-Broadway stuff. He has a background in education and he teaches at an underprivileged school up there. Frankly, he's more interested in that, than in acting, although he enjoys it very much.

CFQ: Ben (Duane Jones) convinces everyone to fight it out upstairs, and then when everybody is dead, he winds up surviving in the cellar he prevented them from taking refuge in. Why was this done?
Romero: It was just another little irony. I mean it was an intentional irony. There was an establishing sequence that keyed that up harder. There wasn't any specific dialogue, but there were some takes that he did. If you noticed, it's a little choppy right at the point where he's going into the cellar and the little girl is coming up. There was realization on his part, but the distributor felt that it wasn't registering so it was cut out.

CFQ: The lighting in the daylight scenes is natural and almost documentary-like, while lighting in the night scenes is very expressionistic. Was this intentional?

Romero: Well, we've talked about that in the mention of my artistic background.

CFQ: What lighting techniques were used?
Romero: That was another thing that was kind of budgetary. In the daylight scenes we just didn't use light, because we used just ambient, natural light.

CFQ: How would the film have been different if it had been made by AIP in Hollywood?
Romero: Well, I don't know. I think that there probably would have been a scientist in the group, explaining what was going on. I think the ending would have been different. In fact, American International turned the picture down on the basis of it being too unmitigated. They told us that if we would reshoot the end of it they would distribute it. Have Ben survive and come out somehow.

CFQ: Do you think artistic and innovative horror films can be made under the Hollywood system where commercial considerations are so pervasive?
Romero: Oh, sure you can. I think you can. Well, I've been trying to walk the line. We're still independent. We've tried to walk the line. I think that our films have been commercial, but at the same time have had some intelligence in them. *Jack's Wife* is an intelligent commentary of what goes on in the mind, yet it's commercial enough that I'm sure, in fact I know, that it's going to be released. In fact, we've had inquiries about it and are negotiating.

CFQ: Your most recent production is *The Crazies*. Are you going to stick with that title?
Romero: I hope to hell not! The original title was *The Mad People*, and I liked that better. Again, that film, as an original story, was written as a pure allegory. The basic premise being that everyone in the world is operating at some level of insanity. You know, the old question, what is sane, what is insane? The device that was used in the story was the accidental spill of a biological weapon into the water supply of a little town, which enabled us to look at people really operating, that is to crystallize this operation of different types of people at varying levels of insanity: And it was again purely an allegory, and the distributors liked it, and I knew immediately when the distributors liked it that they liked the premise and not the allegory, once again. In the rewrite of the

script which I did collaboratively with Lee Hessel, who is distributing the film, we went that way, we went literally, we went plot line with it, although I think again, the allegory is still there.

CFQ: Do you think there is a similarity between *The Crazies* and *Night of the Living Dead*, and if so was this intentional due to the commercial success of your first film?

Romero: No, it really wasn't. We had the basic story which was written by one of our commercial directors here, and the script came out of that. On my draft, my version of the script, I wasn't looking for any intentional similarities at all. I think that some people are gonna say that it has similarities. One of the commanding officers in the film is a black man, and it's the same thing, a band of people trying to survive against this onslaught, in this case, military personnel trying to button up a town. And it does, in that sense, have those similarities, but beyond that the similarity is gone. It's a different commentary altogether.

CFQ: Were you satisfied with the way Continental distributed *Night of the Living Dead*? Would you have done it differently?

Romero: Yes, I would have promoted it a little subtler. I would have understated, that's all. I was a little bit distressed with the way they handled it. I felt that it could have done better. I felt that it could have even done some key run.

CFQ: Have you been approached by any Hollywood studio to do a film?

Romero: With a few offers, not directly from studios. As you say, most of the production is being done independently now. I've been approached by several independents and been written into several proposals, and several of them didn't come through. One of them I turned down, on the basis of being able to do it here.

CFQ: Do you plan on making more horror films?

Romero: I don't know.

CFQ: You're gonna make films?

Romero: Yea, right.

CFQ: The content is not important.

Romero: Not really, no. I have a script I wrote and very much want to do, and I would really like to do *Tarzan* like I mentioned.

CFQ: Which ape call did you prefer, the MGM or the other?

Romero: (laughing) Neither. I didn't like any of them. Didn't sound like an ape. That's what I'd like to do. I'd like to get in touch with Kubrick and get those ape suits. (laughing) And really do the number, or a larger portion of that.

CFQ: It's been so long since anybody has made a good Tarzan.

Romero: It's never been made, I don't think it's ever been made. The closest one was Elmo Lincoln. It came closest to being the "ape man." But that wasn't it. It was off base. It was off target.

Jane should be in it, but Jane should be in it the way Burroughs wrote it. He should come up to the burning mansion in his big limousine and rescue her, in the southern mansion, and bring her off to the jungle.

I think it would have some pertinence today. It's a tremendous little statement in itself, if you want an original hippy. That's what he is and that's the way it should be done. He goes back to the jungle for a sabbatical every once in a while. When he wants to get something off his chest. And he's a beautiful guy. It should be written that way. He's a very intelligent, very glib kind of a man, a man about the world.

CFQ: Would you pick a known actor to play Tarzan?

Romero: Yea. Of course I really don't know. I really don't have any idea. You know, when he was a little younger looking, I think probably Connery would have been pretty good. Like Connery as he looked in *Dr. No* or *From Russia with Love*, probably would have been pretty good looking. I'm just thinking of physical dynamics. I really don't know who would be good.

CFQ: You were, I guess, raised on Weissmuller?

Romero: Yea, right. Weissmuller and then Lex Barker. But they were the same, they were all that Hollywood image, the romanticized image of the ape man who lived in the jungle and who beat up on the baddies who were after the ivory.

CFQ: Do you think you'd have any trouble making a *Tarzan* film with the Black movement being what it is?

Romero: I don't think so.

CFQ: There's the problem of the white ape beating up the blacks.

Romero: No, that doesn't happen very often in the Burroughs stuff really. And when it happens it's no kind of a jab. You know, he's in that society, there are goodies and baddies, and he's in a predominantly black society. I don't think there's really any sweat there at all.

CFQ: Have you ever got into Burroughs fantasy?
Romero: The other stuff, yea. Oh, I'd love to do some of that too.

CFQ: Would you like to do a western?
Romero: Yea, I think I would. Although I used to say what I'm saying about Tarzan now. I used to say they've never made a good western and suddenly, along came *The Wild Bunch* and some of the others that I think have been particularly good. I'd still like to do it, but I guess my interest has been knocked out of me kind of a little bit by seeing some pretty good stuff on the screen. Not from the standpoint that I'm not going to compete with that, but I've lost interest in doing it just for the sake of doing it because it hasn't been done.

CFQ: It would be kind of hard to do in Pittsburgh anyway?
Romero: (laughing) Oh yea . . . I'm a romantic. I'd really like to do just a straight romantic thing.

CFQ: Like your film *The Affair*?
Romero: Well, no. That was a spinoff of the trend at the time. It was another attempt on our part to walk the line. Make something commercial that was trying to be a little bit intelligent too, and that was a spinoff of *The Graduate/Goodbye, Columbus* period and is really all that is and that's all I can say about it, although I think it has a nice light feeling to it.

CFQ: When can we look forward to seeing *Jack's Wife* and *The Crazies* or *The Mad People*, whatever the title may be?
Romero: *The Affair* should be starting to play in New York right about now. *Jack's Wife* is coming out of the lab within a couple of weeks, but by the time that gets sold and a campaign worked on, and everything else, it's going to be quite some time, and I just have no answer on *Jack's Wife*. *The Crazies*, in fact, is going to be out before *Jack's Wife* even though we shot it after *Jack's Wife*, for several reasons. First of all, it was presold. We had the distributor before we produced the film, and in fact, it's a coproduction with the distributor, Cambist Films, which is Lee Hessel. Secondly, it was shot in 35mm and *Jack's Wife* was shot in

16. *Jack's Wife* has yet to be, once it's sold, blown up, whereas *The Crazies*, once I get the cut, we can have a print in a few weeks. I think *The Crazies* will probably be opening sometime, well, he's hoping to open it around Thanksgiving. That might be optimistic, but I would say definitely before the end of the year or right at the end of the year.

CFQ: Do you think *The Crazies* will be a "drive-in" movie like *Night of the Living Dead* was, or will it be an "indoor." Do you think spring or summer would be a better release date for a horror film, or does it matter?

Romero: I don't consider *The Crazies* being a horror film, really. It's science fiction to the extent that *Fail Safe* was science fiction, and things like that, but it's more at that level. It isn't really fantasy. I think that *The Crazies* could go first run easily. I think it will probably have great success in the showcases.

CFQ: I hope it's not going to get saddled to the bottom half of some double-bill. Do you know anything about that?

Romero: I think when they open it—I know he is planning on opening it in New York. I think he is gonna showcase it in New York, but he's really not sure. Of course, he hasn't seen any of it. Depending on what it looks like, he'll either give it a first run, key run situation, or he'll open it showcase, but that's New York, which differs, very often from different parts of the country. I know that in Pittsburgh it will play by itself in a first run house when it first opens. But in New York it is very difficult and very expensive to open a film key run and you can loose your shirt just trying to promote it in the city of New York, and if it duds, it duds, and you've really lost a lot of money and you've got to play a few other cities just to recover that.

CFQ: Then he's not really planning on a world premier in Pittsburgh now?

Romero: I don't know what he's doing. I know he had a miserable failure with *The Affair*, which was then called *There's Always Vanilla* here in Pittsburgh. The same thing happened to us. Our only really bad review was in Pittsburgh on that film and I think it hurt it a little bit here. Everywhere else it has played it has gotten pretty good reviews. I don't know really. That's entirely up to the people who are going to be developing the campaign and promoting it.

CFQ: After viewing the first twenty-five minutes of the rushes on *The Crazies* today all I can say is what a pace! Do you have any idea what your running time will be and what they'll cut it down to?

Romero: I'm shooting for ninety to a hundred. I estimated the script from the jump at about ninety or a hundred and so it'll be somewhere in there. There seems to be a rule of thumb, which I can't really explain, that a film has to be ninety minutes. I think that some distributors feel that if a film goes ninety-one that everyone is gonna get up out of their seats when the sweep hand hits ninety and miss the ending. I really don't understand that. I think if the film holds your interest it's not important.

I've seen this reel we saw today on *The Crazies* about four times. Normally, by about the second or third time I get super critical and I start cringing in my seat while I'm watching the stuff because I know there are things that—and I say to myself: "Christ! Why did I do that! How did I miss that." But this one keeps me cookin'. And that twenty-five minutes rolls and it seems like about ten or fifteen. It's a very brutally paced unrelenting kind of a piece, which is one of the things that I was shooting for, and it deals basically with a commentary on the military.

CFQ: Don't you think television would ruin this if they ever showed it?

Romero: Yea, but I don't know if they could show it. One of our negotiations on the script was with a television outfit that funds and produces those movies for TV. They looked at the script. They really wanted it, but they told us what would have to be done to it, in order to put it on TV.

CFQ: Take out the military and everything else.

Romero: Right. It would have been too tame for what it's saying. The language isn't too heavy and that wouldn't bother me. They may be reluctant because of the subject matter.

CFQ: I don't know if we should discuss the ending at all. That burns the hell out of me when I see an interview about how a movie ends.

Romero: Well, let's not.

CFQ: Could we discuss the ending that was shot or the ending that you had in mind and just say that there's going to be a different ending. Would that suffice, or should we just shut up about it?

Romero: Well, it doesn't bother me. Originally, the town was gonna get wiped out.

CFQ: Would you describe that scene that you had for me at the end? That's what I wanted to get to.

Romero: The romantic leads were to get separated. Nobody knows what's going on. Suddenly the military moves in and—bang!—they're all over the place. As it gradually unfolds you find out that they spilt, because of the Presidential order to dump the bio-weapons, that they deactivated one of the weapons and they were transporting it for dumping and the plane crashed and you find out then that deactivation means only about 98 to 99 percent and therefore there is some active virus in the water supply in the town.

We're dealing with the military people and with the town's people, and were dealing with the two romantic leads of the civies. They get separated and at the very end—the whole time there's a bomber over the town in case the perimeter breaks, because of the possibility of the virus being carried out, there's the chance that they have to bomb the town. We were going to end it with the two lovers, after having been separated, running toward each other and just before they reach each other on the screen, the screen was gonna go white and they were gonna destroy the town with the bomb. But we didn't do that.

George Romero: From *Night of the Living Dead* to *The Crazies*

Fran Lebowitz, Pat Hackett, and Ronnie Cutrone/1973

Originally published in *INTERVIEW Magazine*, April 1973, 30–31, 45. Courtesy of Interview, Inc.

When he was twenty-eight years old, George Romero wrote and directed *Night of the Living Dead*, the black and white horror classic that has terrified even the most sophisticated audiences at midnight shows all over the country for the last two years. He has just completed a new film (in color), *The Crazies*, which is about events in a small Pennsylvania town following the crash nearby of a government plan carrying a virus used in bacteriological warfare.

Question: When one of our writers last interviewed you, you said you were going to make a movie about hippies. Did you?
Romero: About what?

Q: About hippies and what they would be like in a few years. Did you ever make it?
Romero: I don't remember that . . .

Q: Did you make any movies between 1968—*Night of the Living Dead*—and *The Crazies*?
Romero: Yes I did. Two. I think I know what it was. That was probably a misunderstanding. That interview must have been three years ago. When was that?

Q: In 1969. Was *Night of the Living Dead* your first movie?
Romero: My first feature.

Q: Was that a formula with the black hero?
Romero: It was an accident. The whole movie was an accident.

Q: In *The Crazies*, there's a black hero, also.
Romero: Well, in the case of *The Crazies* I wrote the finished screenplay, and the character had been written black originally, so I left it alone. But in *NOTLD* it was purely accidental. The part wasn't written for a black man, but we knew Duane and he was the best guy around for it at the time.

Q: He was perfect.
Romero: Yes, he was perfect. He worked out well. That was accidental. And when we were first screening it for distributors they said, "Well, you ought to throw in some Comment, shoot some more scenes, make a point out of the black guy . . ." Then they wanted to change the ending. They wanted him to survive. In fact, AIP was going to pick the film up if we shot a new ending.

Q: So the two movies that you did in between, what were they like? Did they have pessimistic endings?
Romero: Actually, the second film that we did was probably the one I was talking about when I mentioned hippies, but it turned out the film was nothing like the concept. We were under the thumb of a group of investors in Pittsburgh.

Q: Was it black and white?
Romero: No, color.

Q: 35mm?
Romero: No, 16mm. We shot the second and third films in 16mm. And the third film is . . . uh . . . going to be opening. In fact it just opened in Texas.

Q: What's the name of that?
Romero: Well, our title was *Jack's Wife*. They have changed the title to *Hungry Wives*.

Q: Is it anything like a horror movie, or . . . ?
Romero: It isn't really. It deals with the occult peripherally. It deals with a suburban housewife who gets involved with the occult.

Q: Is there anything pornographic to make them name it *Hungry Wives*?
Romero: No. I don't understand the campaign; I don't understand the ads. Because it's a pretty good film.

Q: Did you look for distributors here for it and everything?
Romero: Yeah. And there wasn't very much interest in it. They just said it was too—wordy.

Q: But after—Is *Night of the Living Dead* considered a commercial success now?
Romero: Yes. It is. There's no question about that. It has done some big numbers. It's still playing here and in a number of places.
Arthur Rubine (press agent): It revived the Midnight Show.

Q (to Arthur): What took it so long to get off the ground?
Romero (to Rubine): You weren't on your own then. You weren't really involved.

Rubine: I was the director of Walter Reade.
Romero: Yeah, but you didn't call those shots.

Rubine: Yes but had I been calling those shots I would have called them all wrong. I mean the first time we all saw *Night of the Living Dead* at Walter Reade, the screening for the whole company was the morning Bobby Kennedy died. You can imagine how much we were into it. When Duane hit the guy in the head with the—Well, at that point we just said, "Fuck this. Who wants to sit through this? Bobby Kennedy just—" We'd all sat up all night listening . . . That was 1968. It opened in Pittsburgh and did a huge business and we brought it to New York and Vincent Canby wrote a paragraph and a half on it. Missing it entirely. *Variety* said it was possibly the worst commercial film ever made . . .
Romero: They got down to the print quality. They said it was printed on Army issue stock or something . . . And then what happened was it got stoned to death by *Reader's Digest*. Roger Ebert in Chicago happened to walk into a theater for a children's matinee and some idiot scheduled *Night of the Living Dead* for a children's matinee. So he walked into the theater and the kids were totally hysterical. They were hysterical with fear. And what happens with children's matinees is that parents drop their children off and then leave. So they're stuck in this theater with

all this murder going on. So Roger wrote a piece not really attacking the picture so much as the people who had shown it to the children, and *Reader's Digest* picked it up and of course re-titled the traditional piece. "What Is Hollywood Doing to Children?" Cited it with two other films, I forget what they were.

Rubine: And then what happened was they showed it in England and the critics went ape. They loved it. And they were lined up in France for weeks. And that's when it started to kick off. *Sight and Sound* did a thing on it and that's when your people at *Interview* picked up on it. There became two or three *Living Dead* freaks among the media. I would get long distance calls form the weirdest places from people dedicating their lives to George Romero. I don't think you guys knew what you had really, did you?

Romero: We didn't really, but—I had an idea. You weren't involved but I remember vaguely some of the cats coming in to Pittsburgh and saying, "We're going to do a real nice job on this." And I said, "Well, I think that it has some merit." In fact, I told them at the time that I thought they could go key run with it, at least in Pittsburgh, to try it. And they weren't interested. They just didn't think that that was where it was at. And I wasn't sure. You know, I didn't know . . . I never expected this kind of reaction after the initial break.

Rubine: Once Canby dismissed the picture so entirely out of hand, we figured what we had was a programmer. You know, you bring it into town, run a big ad the day it opens and you say "Scream-your-guts-out-scare-yourself-to-death" and that's it. Actually I had an idea to do a scream contest and have it in the lobby with a tape recorder, because people walking by would hear the screams and you'd get people to comc in and see it.

Romero: And then there was the life insurance policy.

Rubine: Yes, it was a real one, so we were afraid someone would really have a heart attack in the movie and we'd have to pay it off. And cost us a fortune. We had two days of meetings figuring the odds. Because some guy would come in who would have an attack even if he were watching Doris Day.

Q: Especially if he were watching Doris Day. You have your own production company still, don't you? And you still work out of Pittsburgh?

Romero: Yes, we're still in Pittsburgh. We still do industrial contracts.

Q: Were you born there?

Romero: No, I was born here in New York and I went there to go to school, and I was a painting and design major, but I've always been into film, and I used to make film when I was a kid. My uncle had a set-up you know with the viewer and the little sound system and he used to horse around. And that's how I got into it. And I worked while I was in school. I worked in the union out of New York, and so I was always into it and so a year before I graduated, I transferred out of the drama department, so I graduated out of the drama department and I got involved with a theater group out there and so I stayed there because I was really into that. You know I was just into it with the people who were there and so I just stayed there, didn't bother looking for a job, and so a bunch of us from the theater group got together and decided that we would form a company. There was nothing happening—this was about eleven-twelve years ago, right around the time when television commercials were becoming good in the sense of the craft that was being used to produce them. And there was nothing happening in Pittsburgh. No one shooting any film out there. All it was was a guy standing in front of a camera saying, "This is good." And so we opened up a little shop on the south side of the city and we started to do some film. Spot-work which was foreign to Pittsburgh at the time when people would go to the TV station and hold a product up and smile. And so we had a couple of cameras and some lights and we did everything on location. So we got a rep there as a commercial house, and then that really started to accelerate and the company got pretty big and we started to do some political things and then we started to make some money. We just went around to the advertising agencies there, because there are some big ones there because there's a lot of industry there . . .

Q: So how did you pick horror?

Romero: Well we had a couple of scripts. We started to make some money from commercial things and from political work, and so the company took on a kind of stature, and we—I had two or three scripts I read and wanted to do and—well right after we got out of school we had made a film that we never got so far as marrying a track on . . . it was called *Expostulations* and was made of six vignettes. It's a pretty good film.

Q: That was your first one?

Romero: Yes, this is right out of school. We found an angel who gave us a few thousand dollars and we made this little film called *Expostulations*. But we never even really finished it.

Q: How much did you make *Night of the Living Dead* for?
Romero: Well, the real cash on the line that we had to put in by the time we had the answer print was around $60,000. With the deferred payments and everything it went up to a hundred and twenty . . .

Q: How much has it made?
Romero: I'd like to know. There's a lawsuit somewhere . . .
Rupine: Every time an independent film is picked up, there's a lawsuit.

Q: And *The Crazies*? How much did that cost?
Romero: $250,000.

Q: It looked like it cost more.
Romero: Well, that's because we have the commercial operation facilities there already, so we have our own crew on salary, so we don't have to hire people, we have our own equipment, our own sound equipment, our own 35mm gear, our own lights . . . everything. So it doesn't cost anything. The accountants tell me that I have to amortize it, so somewhere on the P&L statement the cost is there, but it's not really money. Actually, if we were to analyze the cost of that film it's probably $600,000.

Q: So it's just like on the side of a full-scale commercial operation.
Romero: Yes. Well for me, though, it's no longer "on the side."

Q: But as far as the books go.
Romero: The company's called Latent Image and it's an umbrella company. Most of the films are done under separate companies or limited partnerships. The features. We did one on our own. With our own money. It's now called *Hungry Wives*. Formerly titled *Jack's Wife*. And I felt sure that they would pick it up and sell it as a witchcraft thing.

Rupine: Is the ad they're using a soft-core sell?
Romero: Yeah. That's the South. But there's nothing in it. Not even any skin.

Rupine: Maybe they cut something into it.
Romero: No, they did not. I've seen it.

Q: You said there were two movies in between *Night of the Living Dead* and *The Crazies*. What was the other one?
Romero: It was called *There's Always Vanilla*. Which was a real bomb.

Q: What was the subject of that?
Romero: Well, we started— We had an interesting premise. It was going to be what happens to the youth culture in five or ten years but . . .

Q: What happened in the movie?
Romero: Nothing happened in the movie. (laughs) But the idea seemed great.

Q: What was the idea?
Romero: It was going to be a full cycle back-around.

Q: To the parents?
Romero: Yea, to parents. But more than that. I still don't think the film was that bad.
Rupine: It's dated though. The abortion scene is outdated. By the time we screened it there was legal abortion everywhere. And that gets rid of one dramatic scene.

Q: Abortion scenes used to be so scary.
Romero: I still don't think it was that bad.

Rupine: It's that bad.
Romero: Is it really? It can't be.

Rupine: It is. "That bad" means it isn't good enough to get people to leave their houses.
Romero: Oh well okay, then sure. It's that bad. I mean, I consider *Night of the Living Dead* a fluke, so in that sense we were very lucky . . .

Q: Who were the extras?
Romero: That was a great way to save money, because you can't see the faces of the troops in gas masks. I'm sure everybody got killed twelve times.

Q: I remember one scene where there seems to be a lot of people shown in one shot. So I remember thinking that you had bought a lot of white uniforms.

Romero: Yeah, there were quite a few.

Q: The scene where they shot the whole main street of the town.

Romero: Actually there were about thirty guys and there were about four guys that "died." They were good die-ers. We kept shooting them.

Q: Where do you get the special effects on *Night of the Living Dead* and *Crazies*? They were both good.

Romero: Yeah, we have this little guy and he's a maniac, and we're doing a reenactment film for Consolidated Coal on the Blackstone Mine disaster, and we have to create a mine fire, and this cat is working on that, and I don't want to be down in that shaft with him when he does it. That guy's a maniac. You should have seen him on the sets for *Crazies*. He smokes a cigar, it's always lit, he's working with explosives, and he and his buddy toss the stuff around like it's nothing and they're working with a jelly, that kind of plastic explosive and they're planting charges all over the trees. And they would do it for kicks! We'd be walking across the set and they'd have things wired into trees . . . Maniacs . . . Very creative guys. They have a fireworks company out there. This has always been their bag.

Q: When Clank gets shot in the head, when the blood spurts straight out, it looked real.

Romero: We came up with that at the very last minute because Hal was sick and we shot on the very last day he was there, and so when he wasn't there for a couple of days and so what do you do in a town that small. So I was wandering around and I went to a sporting goods store and got a bunch of components and made an extra hairpiece for him and so we couldn't use a charge on his head, so we had to—Well if it's on the body, if it's under clothing or under something it's done with an explosive. But this was on his head so we just made another piece of hair and we made up the wound first and made it look like a wound, and then we ran a tube into the wound and then down into his jacket and he squeezed and the blood came out of the tube. So then we made up an extra piece of hair to put over the wound which was already a wound and so when the gun went off we pulled the hair off which it's so fast you can't see it.

Q: What were the intestines in *Night of the Living Dead*? Just animals?
Romero: Yes. One of the investors was a meat packer. That's true. He dug it. He wanted a credit.

Q: But these people who make explosives, they're in Pittsburgh too?
Romero: They have a fireworks company.

Q: And yours are the only movie effects that they do?
Romero: Yeah. They really get off on it. We've shot a lot of effects just for fun . . .

Q: What kind of movies do you like?
Romero: Unfortunately, I don't get up to New York as much as I'd like. I've been tied up editing *The Crazies* at home for so long. Unfortunately nothing plays in Pittsburgh—twelve theaters—and not too much gets there, so I miss a lot. We were lucky to get *Slaughterhouse* . . . and I kind of like *Deliverance*.

Q: What are you going to do next?
Romero: Just marking time. We have a couple of properties we're considering and I have a script I'm working on.

Q: Things that you've written yourself or that you've worked on with other people?
Romero: That I've written myself. On *The Crazies* I did an adaptation.

Q: Was *Night of the Living Dead* your own?
Romero: I wrote *Night of the Living Dead* as a short story, which strangely enough was an allegorical thing, but then when we did the film, the allegory went out. But not entirely. It did go out of my mind, though.

Rupine: The Europeans picked up the allegory. Anubis is an Egyptian god who is someday supposedly going to lead the dead against us. And that's what we originally called the picture—*Night of Anubis*. No, we called it *Enubis*, and they said no one would know who he was.
Romero: We tried for a couple of years to interest some Pittsburgh money into doing a film and we couldn't get anywhere and so we said, "Well, we're going to go out and we're going to do a real guts thing and we'll do it for as sure a market we can shoot it for.

Q: Do you think you'll ever do a movie in black and white again?
Romero: I really like it. I like it much better than color, generally.

Q: Why did you do *The Crazies* in color?
Romero: Well I don't know that you can sell a black and white any more.

Q: It's a great title.
Romero: I didn't like it at first. It was Lee's title.

Q: I love it. We've been all telling **** how much she resembles the doctor in the movie. He was very well cast.
Romero: He's an incredible guy. He's not an actor. His name is Richard France. He's now at the University of Rhode Island. He has never acted before.

Q: Who was David?
Romero: W. G. McMillan.

Q: Is he an actor?
Romero: He is an actor, but I don't know that he's ever done anything of this scope before. He was an extra in the film and we had to replace the lead about four days into shooting and that's how Mac got the part. It was a real Cinderella story. He wasn't even able to maintain his SAG status. I don't think he's ever made more than two grand a year as an actor.

Q: I saw the guy who plays the first officer to arrive in the town in a commercial on TV last night.
Romero: Lanacaine, right? "Jesus, do I itch!"

Q: Did the army help you?
Romero: We didn't get Jeep One from the military. We asked them for technical information on the development of the weapon and we wanted just some information on rank and behavior and martial law and stuff like that and they did send us some books and were going to work with us, apparently, but it came down to a long, drawn-out stall, so we gave up. We needed some military advice just procedurally and it was a weird thing. The high school in the town has an ROTC program in the high school and there's a guy there named Garrett who is

a retired colonel or something and he is Militarist Number One and he runs ROTC for the kids. And a lot of the soldiers are these ROTC kids. He said, "Well, I really don't like the idea of the film, but . . . ah . . . sometimes we have to—look aside. And my boys, I like to get them off to camp every summer and they could use a contribution . . ." and so that's the way it worked out.

Q: Did the town cooperate?
Romero: They shut us down for a week because of the incest scene which wasn't at all graphic, but they shut us down. They saw it in the script. They locked us out of the high school.

Q: How do you think it'll be rated?
Romero: I would think GP. You have to get a rating or else you get an X around the country. Self-imposed. Van Peebles may test the law, not ask for a rating, on his next picture.

Q: Because you yourself have to pay yourself to get yourself a rating?
Rupine: Yes.
Romero: Don't you think ratings really do affect you? Subliminally?
Rupine: I always avoid G movies.

Morning Becomes Romero

Dan Yakir/1977

From *Film Comment* 15, no. 3 (1977): 60–65. Reprinted by permission.

With *Dawn of the Dead*, George A. Romero emerges from the midnight circuit—where he has reigned for the last decade with his *Night of the Living Dead*—as a true auteur. *Dawn of the Dead* is Romero's break-through film in which his subversive, unsentimental and truly original vision is focused—with blood, guts, and humor—on our consumer society gone mad. Using the quick pace and the high-adventure format of *The Crazies*, Romero recreates the cannibalistic zombies that have become his trademark since *Night of the Living Dead*.

Romero is undoubtedly the most important regional filmmaker working in the U.S. From his Pittsburgh headquarters he has made six independently produced films since 1968, often serving as writer and editor as well. He has redefined the genre film like nobody could. After *Dawn of the Dead,* the horror film will never be the same.

Dan Yakir: How did the concept of the "Living Dead" first strike you? And how did it develop into *Dawn of the Dead*?

George Romero: I read a book called *I Am Legend* by Richard Matheson and got very much into the socio-political through-line that's present in it, although it doesn't really follow through. Inspired by it, I wrote a short story which dealt with a revolutionary society coming into being in the form of a zombie society—people coming back to life as soon as they die—and it was a trilogy right from the jump. In Part I, they appear, but operative society seems to be staying on top of it, even though there's a lot of chaos and people don't know how to handle it. In Part II, there's an equal balance, with the outcome undecided. In the Third Part, it's the zombies who are operative. I have this vision of a layered society where the humans are little dictators, down in bomb shelters, and they fight their wars using zombies as soldiers. The operative humans have to be out feeding the zombies, controlling them and keeping law and order. In that layer of society we'll ultimately get our hope; those are the characters we'll be able to care about. It's a return to what the zombie was in the beginning: Lugosi always lived in a castle while the zombies went out to pick the sugar cane.

It's Part I that we turned into *Night of the Living Dead*: the new society appears and attacks every aspect of our society and all the mores down to religion and concepts about death. People don't really know how to deal with it other than just defend themselves. The scientific community has absolutely no answers. The radiation scenario that people feel is an explanation in *Night of the Living Dead* was actually one out of three that were advanced in the original cut of the film, but the other ones got cut out and people have adopted that radiation thing as the reason why the dead are coming back. I really didn't mean that to be.

So, in *Dawn of the Dead* I was careful to avoid any explanation of the phenomenon.

After making *Night of the Living Dead*, I went through a paranoid phase of not wanting to be a horror moviemaker, which is why my next two films were not horror films: *There's Always Vanilla* and *Jack's Wife*. I resisted even developing a second part into a sequel. Then, gradually, as I became comfortable with what *Night of the Living Dead* was and with what my reputation was, I finally got the idea for it. It was four years ago. I saw Monroeville Mall, with its Civil Defense area up above. And Mark Mason, one of the owners, told me he had always had this fantasy about some hermit living up there, who could have anything he wanted. That gave me the idea that it was the perfect setting for the equal-balance part of the trilogy.

So, I wrote a treatment and it was very heavy, ponderous, possessing roughly the same attitude as *Night of the Living Dead*. But then I realized that the place itself, the mall, was too funny to serve for a nightmare experience. *Dawn of the Dead* is a nightmare, but it's more a pop fantasy than a brooding nightmare—which *Night*, with all its funny scenes, was.

You can't use the word "camp" anymore, but that's what we were doing then and still doing. We're just calling it something else, I guess. Camp has come to mean something disrespectful, but I wasn't trying to be disrespectful of the genre. I was just trying to indicate some of the things that were going on within it.

Dawn of the Dead is very much upfront; *Night* more insidious. Now we can laugh at it, but when the film first came out, most of Middle

America was scared watching it. In *Night*, I was going for a real, traditional horror-movie scare, rather than intellectual fear. *Dawn of the Dead* has some startles, but if you come out of it afraid, it's purely on an intellectual plane. It's not really frightening. I meant it to be kind of exuberant. And the battle that develops over Revlon and Charmain and whatever treasures they believe they've found takes the trappings from the traditional genre and puts it in high adventure—a mixture of weird pop with the fantastic.

DY: What's the difference between fantasy violence and real violence?
GR: The fantasy violence in *Dawn of the Dead* is just a texture. You come to accept it like the violence in *San Antonio* with Errol Flynn, where the gun battles go on for thirty minutes: It doesn't have the effect of the violence in say, *Taxi Driver*, where we're watching a real person getting his hands on a gun and we go through the whole range of emotions of what it means to have that power and think about killing someone. That's where I draw the difference. I object more to the blood and violence in something like *Every Which Way But Loose*, in which Clint Eastwood travels around the country, beating up on people. Quantifiably there's less blood than in *Dawn of the Dead*, but it's this kind of cavalier violence that has an effect on the street.

I don't think fantasy violence ever had a similar effect. Within the fantasy context I prefer to see the blood. I refuse to cut away from it. I want to plant the idea firmly in the mind of the audience, make them understand what the threat to the characters is. There were photographers in *Look* magazine showing little kids in Beirut and Ireland playing execution games. Kids imitate violence that they're exposed to in media or real life, but they'll adopt it as a viable behavior only if they see it as a rehearsal for what their life is going to be. Otherwise, when a kid imitates Superman, he imitates him doing a violent act, because kids are the most frustrated members of society. They ain't nothin' yet and they know it and they'd like to at least pretend to behave assertively and aggressively.

DY: What is it that attracts you to the horror-fantasy genre?
GR: It was a genre I enjoyed as a child. I grew up on EC comic books and went to see all the fifties horror films, the B movies. Since I wasn't an athlete, I wasn't a very popular kid in school. My few close friends and I were living in our own little fantasy world. Beyond that, it was really a matter of being able to sell it. Before *Night of the Living Dead*,

which was my first theatrical film, I tried to sell a couple of scripts that were not genre pieces at all and, of course, couldn't get any support. So, ten of us got together and put in six hundred bucks apiece and bought a case of film and rented the farmhouse and started shooting. I never expected *Night* to become what it did, but it got me a reputation in the genre, so it's been easier for me to sell such projects. I think there's been a great deal of acceptance of the genre in the last few years and I no longer have the old paranoia. I'm more relaxed and I enjoy it more now. And it's an easy way to tell parables with my kind of a fantasy.

DY: Parables that have a comic-book format?
GR: Yes. On the surface, I was doing popular genre stuff, but I always feel when there's no linear thread underneath it all. Fantasy has always been used as parable, as socio-political criticism: *Alice in Wonderland*, *Gulliver's Travels* . . . I love the Japanese Godzilla films. They're not scary at all, but as a phenomenon born out of the war, the bomb, they say more to me than *Hiroshima, Mon Amour*. So, I insist on having that underbelly.

When I write a script, that's what I think about first. After I have it in my head, I can write the script in two weeks, because the surface doesn't matter: the characters can behave any way you want them to. But you have to know where you're going. In the sixties we used to sit around in coffee shops and talk and solve all the problems of society and filmmakers did it in their movies. We don't do that anymore. Films are still critical of society, but this criticism has taken the form of parables communicated through the fantasy film. I do it in very broad strokes, with a comic-book type humor and extreme staging and a very pedantic kind of structure. But the socio-political parable is to me like a handshake with the audience. I don't think I'm saying anything new: it's a wink and should be taken as such.

DY: Don't you think the dead in your films would be more frightening if they were indistinguishable from the living?
GR: That's the concept of the *Body Snatchers*—and I didn't find the new version particularly frightening. *Night of the Living Dead* is more frightening because it's in black-and-white. There's nothing about the make-up that tips you right away. However, you know a zombie once you see one. It's more frightening also because it's more banal. It's the neighbors. In *Dawn of the Dead* my concept was to make them a little klutzy, so I gave them these broad types—an Air Force general, a nun, a

hare krishna—people from all walks of life. You get startled when one of them jumps from behind the boiler, but there's no buildup of fear.

DY: What do the zombies represent?

GR: As Peter in *Dawn of the Dead* says, "They're us." All the monsters we've created in fiction, unless expressly identified as the Devil, represent our own evil. We create them so we can kill them off, thereby justifying ourselves—it's a kind of penance, self-exorcism. I like the zombies. The monster has traditionally been sympathetic. I always have the image from *Bride of Frankenstein*: of the monster sitting with the little blind man. You have to be sympathetic with the creatures because they ain't doin' nothin'. They're like sharks: they can't help behaving the way they do.

There's an extraordinary incident that happened in Scotland in the fifteenth century, which I've considered making into a film. A man named Sonny Bean and a woman were highwaymen and hid in a cave and they were knocking people off on the road without getting anything, because the economy was in a downslide. The penalty for highway robbery was so extreme that they took to bringing the bodies into the cave and hiding them. Since they weren't getting anything, they took to eating the bodies. There were three generations, all born out of the original couple, when they were finally found—over fifty beings living in this cave, in the back of which they had a larder of human meat. When they were found by the king's army, there were fourth generation little infants for whom it was a way of life. What were they guilty of? Anyway, the army dragged them into the town square and had a four-day orgy of decapitation and burning.

DY: Your vision is not exactly optimistic.

GR: My films pose perhaps a pessimistic view, but I don't consider myself a pessimist. In *Dawn of the Dead* I think there's an optimistic perspective. The fact that the characters, Peter and Fran, finally opt to survive, instead of just giving up, is hopeful. The devastation and the apocalyptic massacre in the mall are there, but there's also an escapist attitude through the film.

DY: You're involved in all aspects of your films: the scenario construction, the dialogue writing, the shooting, the editing. Does each of these phases give you pleasure?

GR: My big hobby is puzzles—math puzzles, brain-teaser books—and I love the ironic ones where the answer is so obvious that you don't find it for two weeks. That's the way I like to think and when I write a script I tend to lean that way too. Creating the plot line is like doing a jigsaw puzzle, making things fit. That's the stuff I play with—I like to use little plot intricacies, details, incidental things happening . . .

But I don't like writing the dialogue. I've always had a tremendous insecurity about writing. I had a Catholic upbringing, movies were an untouchable thing that went on in Hollywood, and I went to parochial schools through high school. Carnegie Tech, Pittsburgh, was the first time I was away from home and I realized I was an individual, let alone that I had my own desires—to make movies. All of a sudden, I got really tenacious. For two years I studied painting and design and in the third year I bought with some friends the rights to *The Connection* by Jack Gelber and I acted in it. Some people from the drama department said I should switch departments. That's when I became convinced that, as Martin says, "it's not magic."

Right after school, we set up our own company. It was a good time and a lucky one for us because there wasn't that much happening around Pittsburgh at that time, so we became "hot commercial shots." We were the first company that was doing film-form commercials, and, for a long time, we were the only game in town. That's where I got the technical side of my experience. Coming from such background, to me it's like learning to use the pencil. I still feel like I'm playing around with the pencil and learning how to draw. I think it's still hard for me to get rid of all those inadequacies that I felt from that kind of upbringing. And I feel very self-conscious when I'm writing something. I think, "Why should people listen to me?" I have to force myself.

DY: In *Martin*, how do you subvert the vampire genre and why?
GR: I don't think I'm trying to subvert it. Someone asked me, "Are you exploding the genre or expanding it?" I don't mean to explode it. The thing that motivated me to do *Martin* was that there were certain points of logic that bothered me—not the least of them being if such a character, a vampire, existed from the beginning of time, he'd really have a tough time today because he'd have to get a new ID every twenty years or so. I mean, a vampire today would really have some sweats.

The vampire is a character that we created so that we can drive a stake through its heart, thereby cleanse our own souls. I took a character out of the traditional myth, a twenty-year-old character who believes he's a vampire since he drinks blood, but who may not be a supernatural character. I don't believe he's eighty-four years old. I think those are things that have been drummed into him from infancy by people like his grandfather Cuda. So, he's a victim and when he tries to explain his problem, the people around him don't listen or don't take him seriously. His neighbor, Mrs. Santini, just wants to get laid, so she uses Martin. Martin is very honest and open about his problem when he calls the radio talk-show, but the talk-show host just says, "Great! Keep calling!"

The setting to me signifies that, for a traditional vampire, the old days are gone: the industrial pride is gone, the jobs are gone, the church is collapsing. Everyone is just surviving. The disintegration is so evident around Pittsburgh. The little mill towns that used to be thriving, proud communities are gone with the wind. It made one of those towns, Braddock, the perfect setting for this kind of situation.

DY: Let's talk about Martin's sexual repression and his disorientation when he finally has sex with a consenting woman.

GR: Martin believes that he needs blood to survive. He doesn't relate it totally to a sexual act, but it's there and he prefers it that way. But when he finally gets into a relationship with Mrs. Santini, he becomes disoriented because he's got a person to relate to and it throws him off stride. He says that all he wants is "the sexy stuff" that real people have, which must be great—he has some misconceptions as to what that's about. That's what screws him up as a killer more than as a vampire. It threatens his behavior as a killer. He's no longer efficient.

DY: Why the lack of emphasis on eroticism in your films? Even the "sexy stuff" in *Martin* is not particularly erotic.

GR: Eroticism, even more than humor, is a very personal kind of thing. I don't see how you can do something erotic and expect it to telegraph to everybody. I have yet to see an explicit sex film that to me is in any way erotic. One of the most erotic scenes to me was in a bad film called *The Brothers Karamazov* where Maria Schell does a dance with two wool sweaters on, in a tavern as Yul Brynner plays the guitar. It's a big schmaltz, but what she does with that little dance is incredibly erotic. But if I said that to somebody, he'd say, "Huh?"

DY: Would you say that *Martin* is a more personal film?

GR: Yes. To me, it's a much more human story, about one-on-one human relationships and I approached it with a different tone—more subtly and more seriously.

I love *Martin*, because I enjoy working with small details. The attack in the house, when Martin discovers Sarah Venable with Al Levitsky—I love that. It all has to do with doorknobs, telephones, stairways . . .

DY: Would you prefer to make films in this vein?
GR: I'm also a sucker for high adventure. The mall in *Dawn of the Dead* struck me as a high-adventure area; there are even jungles in it! And all those guns and weapons and using the car in it—it's *The Dirty Dozen* coming to Monroeville. I like to execute this stuff more than the brooding scary things. I didn't have as much fun making *Martin*. We all knew what we were doing but it wasn't fun to do, because the controls were much tighter. With the action sequences in *Dawn of the Dead* it was pure fun. I felt as if there were no restraints, like running free with all your senses. I'm not a speed freak, but I've had that sensation in a car in an open road late at night when you don't have to worry about signs or anything else. That's exactly what doing action stuff is like—I pull all the stops out, shoot a lot of film and just have fun with it.

The film I'd probably like to make the most—and this is just pure childhood fantasy—is *Tarzan*. When I was a kid Tarzan was my main man. I've read all twenty-three Burroughs books . . .

DY: The bourgeois house, in *Martin*, with all its comforts, becomes as much a deadly trap as the shopping mall in *Dawn*.
GR: Exactly. I like that. And I like the way the place looked: the metallic wallpaper, that pristine look. I was introducing the geography for the first five minutes while flashing back to the scene in Martin's fantasy castle. There's something I like very much about the black-and-white checkered patterns in the fantasy castle as they relate to the metallic silver patterns in the modern place. I love the way it's playing against itself. He goes up the stairs and the spiral staircase of the castle relates to this little carpeted claustrophobic stairway.

DY: What's the difference in effectiveness between the horror potential of color and black-and-white? In that respect, why the graininess in *Martin*?
GR: I don't know how much we can really perceive a different aesthetic from black-and-white. Instead, we get an automatic, nostalgic response

to the great movies we've seen in black-and-white. I think we're only responding to that tradition. That's what happens to me. It puts me in a whole different frame of mind because I can remember sitting in the Loew's American in the Bronx as a kid.

The color in *Martin*—I don't think it interferes at all. My cinematographer, Mike Gornick, did a great job. He used reversal stock instead of negatives, so he was able to get saturation and wash it down. We wanted it to be seedier and there's no great difference between some of those color sequences, particularly in Braddock, and the black-and-white. In fact, we had to push the black-and-white sequences further to make them grainier and grittier than the color ones.

The color in *Dawn of the Dead* is shopping-mall pop. It needs to be different. A lot of people work in color and practice what I call the state of the art gamesmanship. Eastman comes out with a new stock and you can shoot at candlelight and let the windows bleed. Who said it's attractive to let the light bleed through a window? Sometimes it works, but how many times does it really enhance a scene? In *The Godfather* films it does, because you don't know what's outside this bright window. But to do it because "it's a good-looking shot"? Nonsense! It becomes laziness. What is initially a technical advantage becomes the state of the art.

The problem with the movie industry is that it costs so much money and the time-money equation brings so much pressure. So many producers won't rely on something as mystical as someone's desire to make a film, someone's creativity. They need to quantify everything. That's why movies are looking more and more like TV instead of the other way. It used to be that TV was trying to grow up and look like movies, but now it's got so much power that it's dragging the movies with it. So many people in movies are just working, simply doing their job!

DY: Being an independent gives you full control.
GR: It does. I would insist on that. I don't reject the studio system out of hand. I'd like to be able to work with that kind of budget, but I would insist on enough control. It always amazes me why they would hire you at all to take your controls away from you. It doesn't make any sense. I've been in an independent situation all along. None of the features I've made cost serious money until *Dawn of the Dead*. I've never made a film for over $300,000 until *Dawn*, which cost $1.5 million. Richard Rubinstein, the producer, had enough faith in me to say, "Go

do it." Because of my documentary background and the fact that I grew up as a contract producer, I respect that there's only so much money and I'm not going to have a crew sitting around for the sun to appear through the trees. It has to go both ways. There's a lot of mistrust in the industry. The real reason why budgets are so high is not inflation or unions. It's just that nobody would take a gamble. Everybody wants to get their money up-front.

If you're working with $8 million and you have a story board and wonder how much the shark will cost, if something occurs to you and it's not in the story board, you can't do it because it's not in the budget. I love to have flexibility, so I can throw in something that occurs to me. I'd hate to have somebody developing an $800,000 shark for me. I'd go to a costume-maker to make me a rubber shell, I'll put a couple of divers in it and there's a shark! Now let's make the movie!

DY: Are you satisfied with *The Crazies*?
GR: I think maybe it was a little ahead of its time. At the time I made it, we were still in Vietnam and it was a very heartfelt problem, a part of the national consciousness and I don't think anyone was ready to see that situation—even though it's not a Vietnam film, it's an anti-military film. People weren't ready to look at it in a comic-book context. That's my . . . not an error, really, but wrong timing. It was a little too ambitious, a little too rushed. I should have taken out some of the plot incidents and dealt with the rest in a more linear way, with a little more time and space. It's very staccato, which I like at times, but I need a breather from it every once in a while. Aside from that, it needed to be a little longer. The distributor insisted on cutting about fifteen minutes and I didn't have any say about that. I made the cut but had nothing to say about the final running time.

The distributor misinterpreted what the film was about. I still think that the film could have gone out into the drive-ins—it's a potboiler, a B movie, an action melodrama, at least on the surface—and it needed to be played that way. And he thought it was *Jaws* and was going to make a lot of money. He spent a lot of bread opening it in New York in two East Side houses and two Times Square houses, and it didn't survive a week. Then it got shelved. There was no way to revive it, which is another unfortunate reality of the business. We sold it to TV and some European territories. People are actually asking to book it now, but it's not because of it but because of *Martin* and *Dawn of the Dead*.

DY: We haven't spoken about *There's Always Vanilla* and *Jack's Wife*.
GR: Not too many people have ever spoken about those. The first one was *Vanilla* and we shouldn't have made it. *Night of the Living Dead* was making money immediately, even though all we were getting was bad ink. Roger Ebert wrote a pan that *Reader's Digest* picked up and people were saying, "Look at this shit! How far will people go to make a buck!"

Vanilla is *The Graduate*, it's *Goodbye, Columbus*, a romantic comedy about a young musician coming back from the "big time" where he never made it to a Middle-American city—which happens to be Pittsburgh—while the woman is on her way out. It's about their relationship. He's coming back to conformity and she's loosening out, influenced by growing liberalism and music and everything that was happening then. It's dated now, but it's fun to watch, and it looks great. I felt insulted because *Night of the Living Dead* was getting all this bad print—they said it looked like it was printed on army stock—I got crazy about that, so I made *Vanilla* look Hollywood.

Vanilla was picked up for distribution. I've made six films and they've all been distributed. I haven't realized how lucky I was.

Then I went into *Jack's Wife*, which was underwritten by a brokerage and there was a financial disaster. It went belly-up and we were stuck, because we had already borrowed the money to get rolling. Again, it was a little ambitious. I'd like to do a remake of it one day. I really liked the script. It's closest to *Martin* in tone and attitude. It's about a comfortable suburban housewife married to an attorney. She's got everything she could possibly want, except a life. She's one of the ladies in the neighborhood who do everything together, from playing bridge to going out and painting the ghetto. Well, there's a woman in the next community who claims to be a real witch and the ladies get into that. Joan, the housewife, starts doing all these private little rituals at home and believes she's hexing herself into the new lifestyle, but then she starts thinking that what she's doing is evil, but that she's addicted to it. She takes a lover and believes she's becoming a bad person, a tool of the Devil. She's afraid it's the Devil who's making her do it. She winds up going bananas.

Jack Harris picked the film up and called it *Hungry Wives*—"Caviar in the kitchen, nothing in the bedroom!"—and tried to make it look like a soft-core porn movie. But there's no skin in it. It's one of those ridiculous things that I'll never understand.

DY: About your editing technique: in *Dawn of the Dead*, you prefer short scenes for shock effect, with lots of close-ups.

GR: The editing is a part of the pace. In *Martin*, there are some very long, placid sequences, except in the attack scene in the house—and even within it there are some longer shots than in *Dawn of the Dead*. *Dawn* is frenetic, like *The Crazies*. It's built into the direction. I don't like master shots, because I think that when you're trying to make an active scene, you should make the eye move and the cuts move—they should be active as well. It's all part of that subliminal feeling. So, when I do an action scene, I'll shoot it from several different angles, then go in and shoot close-ups, so that I'm really flexible, so that I can cut it anywhere I want, which you can't when you have a master shot.

When I make a first cut on something, I don't just cut the voice and the picture. I'll put in sound effects if they're critical, even music. I also work on a table, not a Moviola or a flat bed. I just work with a synchronizer because I like to see six or eight tracks across the table. There's something very tactile about seeing all those elements. Sometimes I'll play movie soundtracks while I'm cutting, to really lock myself into the mood for a scene. You see, I'm basically a sucker for movies, and I need all these artificial stimuli. I like scoring. A lot of people say my scoring is too heavy, but that's the way I like it. I like Eric Wolfgang Korngold. I want every frame scored, so there's no chance of misinterpreting.

Actually that's not really true: I will get into ironies. I had to fight battles over the ending of *Dawn of the Dead*, because everyone said, "Here's this climactic sequence and you're playing a polka?!"

The George Romero Interview

Richard Lippe, Tony Williams, and Robin Wood/1979

Interview conducted at the Toronto Film Festival, September 15, 1979. Originally published in *Cinema Spectrum* 1 (1980): 4–7. Also present was Richard Rubinstein, producer of *Martin* and *Dawn of the Dead*. Reprinted by permission.

George Romero: I grew up in New York City and went to college in Pittsburgh. Right out of school I started a small contract directing company, doing commercials, industrial films, and so forth. In 1966–67 we started to try interesting investors in putting up money to make a theatrical feature film but they said, "You can't make a theatrical feature film in Pittsburgh!" So I had written a story inspired by Richard Matheson's *I Am Legend* and we decided that we could turn it into a horror film. Ten of us put up $600 apiece, rented a farmhouse and started to shoot. When we showed rushes to people they saw that the lip movements synchronized with the sound and said, "It does look like a movie after all!" So we were able to raise the rest of the money which came to $70,000. From the income we paid off some of the crew and actors so the total budget of *Night of the Living Dead* was $114,000. It took nine and a half months to shoot because we would film for two weeks and then go back and make a beer commercial.

When your first film comes out one has a naive impression of the whole business and we felt that we could keep sitting here in Pittsburgh. So we promptly went out and made a film, *It's Always Vanilla*, for $100,000. Money fell out of the trees because *Night of the Living Dead* was so successful. But the moment the industry found out it wasn't a horror film nobody wanted to screen it anymore. It did get very limited distribution but it never made any money. Then we made *Jack's Wife* for $170,000 but the distributor changed the title to *Hungry Wives* and cut it so it was a pretty disappointing experience. Then we co-produced *The Crazies*. This was all in a matter of four years—'68 to '71—with an independent New York distributor for $274,000 with them putting up half and Pittsburgh private investors putting up the other. When they saw the film they thought they had *Jaws*, and felt they could really make money on it. They misinterpreted what it was and tried to open it in two East Side houses in Times Square, spending a lot of money on the campaign but only twenty-four people showed up at the theatre. That was when Richard Rubenstein and I became partners. After those disappointing experiences I realized that we had to make an effort to find out what the business was. Four years after that we spent the time building our own companies. We did about thirty shows for TV, a lot of import work on European products in the States and we used that as a kind of "entrée" to meet the distributors. Then we began to put together our deal on *Dawn of the Dead* (UK title *Zombies*) which was a much bigger deal than we'd ever done before. It was $1.5 million.

In the meantime I had the idea for *Martin*. Because of what we'd been doing for TV production we made money for our investors, so Richard and I went out to raise the budget for *Martin* which was $250,000, so while we were waiting for the *Dawn* deal to come through we made *Martin*.

Richard Rubenstein: Not many people are aware of George's experience in sports documentaries. We did a series of fifteen one-hour profiles. We were lucky in that we were involved with people who happened to be winners and at the documentary level we had a tremendous time.

GR: I grew up with documentary film. That's when I learned to play around with celluloid.

The style of the shows for American network TV was different from any of the shows which had been done before.

RR: George did them in a montage style which is probably closer to the Wiseman documentaries. There was no voice-over narration. Inter-cut interviews and everybody speaking for themselves had not been seen on U.S. network sports programs before.

Robin Wood: I like your "unknown" films, *Jack's Wife* and *The Crazies*.

GR: I'd like to remake *Jack's Wife* so I'd be able to show it! No, I'm very happy with it. But I would be interested in making a new production deal with the same script.

RW: Where did you get the idea for *Jack's Wife*?

GR: That was my idea. I did some reading about witchcraft for another project I was working on. At the time I was doing some things for public TV in Pittsburgh. A lot of the people surrounding me there were these suburban women. Feminist awareness was beginning. These all came together when I did the script.

I categorize *The Crazies* and *Dawn* stylistically as being in the same family and *Jack's Wife* and *Martin* similarly. *Night of the Living Dead* was just kind of wild, a lot of frustrations were coming out. It has its own kind of technique which is more documentary.

Richard Lippe: In *Jack's Wife* there is a predominant use of dreams and fantasy and it seems that the heroine is creating her own truth rather than there's any hidden truth to find.

GR: She creates her own fantasy. Martin has been formed by the same kind of thing. People suggesting things.

RL: In *Martin* you play much more with horror film conventions. Was that something which intrigued you in *Jack's Wife* that you intended to explore?

GR: I didn't really explore all that much in *Jack's Wife*. There was witchcraft but that wasn't one of the topical themes of the film. *Martin* was much more horror. Some of it was due to confidence with the media. In *Martin* I wasn't afraid to run those three or four planes together. Similarly with *Dawn*. I was a lot more willing just in terms of playing around with that shuffle. That's one problem I had with *Jack's Wife*.

RW: Gregg, in the film, describes her belief in being a witch as a cop-out. One could also link that to Martin. In both cases it prevents a character from confronting social realities and any commitment to changing society. Being a vampire is a very personal solution and not really a very good one on the personal level.

GR: Martin's problem is a little more severe. It's the same problem as Jack's wife but just a little further, if you read it in that way. I think Martin is beyond that. He's not conscious of salvation until the end which is inevitable. She seems to be left with some kind of understanding. *Martin* is on a different plane but that'd be because I needed Martin to believe that he was a vampire.

RW: Within their communities they're both non-persons. Joan is just "Jack's wife." Martin is a nobody. Nobody ever respects or cares for him. Being a witch or a vampire is creating a false identity.

GR: Being an executive relates to that as well!

RL: Did you feel more sympathy for Martin than Joan because of the ending of *Martin* when he comes up with the idea that he might be normal?

GR: Yes, because I kept getting pissed off with Joan and with myself and I know that I didn't put quite enough information in for the audience to be sympathetic towards her. We had a rigid shooting schedule and a lot of pressures put on us by people who had the money, more restrictions, I think, than *Dawn*.

RW: In your films the attitude to religion seems very clear, but in *The Crazies* you have two scenes with animal imagery: the young girl with the sheep (associating her with sacrificial death?) and the snake coming out of the log towards one of the men. What are they doing there?

GR: The first refers to an incident somewhere in Utah or Nevada in 1971 when sheep were contaminated with bacteriological warfare. There were thousands killed. It was one of those big incidents that had people screaming, and the snake showed up! It came out of the log so I took a shot of it.

RR: I have my own theories. George had a very staunch Catholic upbringing and I think he's getting back for every day he had to go to school!

RW: The film's craziness appears to be not merely insanity but the logical expression of aggressive desires which normal life very, very precariously represses. What the drug does is to release, e.g., an old woman's desire to stab someone with a knitting needle that symbolizes domestic slavery. Is this how you see the film?

GR: I was operating more on what the word "normal" means because clearly a lot of people are not affected by the drug. They're caught up in their own actions which do come out of, possibly repression, though the way they've had to live with people in a small town like that, (or just reacting waiting for something to happen) gives them an excuse to behave in that way.

RW: At times we can't tell who's crazy or not throughout the film. At the end it becomes quite uncertain.

GR: It becomes useless to figure out who is infected in the laboratory when they try to find someone who is immune. In the end when they drag the hero in they figure him for some kind of crazy. They're not very intelligently aware of it. He's the only person in the film who *might be* OK.

RL: Do you see too much emphasis put on science in our culture since movie scientists are usually discredited?

GR: I have a strange thing about that which might be autobiographical. They create tools and technology and expect it to be something else. They can't really explain what they did. When I say, "autobiographical" I feel like those scientists when you ask me some of those questions because when I made this film many of the things I put in were instinctive. But five years later I can sit down and start pulling things apart. Yet I'm really at a loss to explain exactly what I did. That's what I'm trying to do with the scientists in *The Crazies*. He has the knowledge but the MPs just put him on the plane and the poor guy is really not aware of what he has created. He's been programmed to use his knowledge only for the purpose of the mechanism.

RW: Both *Night* and *Crazies* have as central components the break-down of the nuclear family. In *Night* Karen eats her father and hacks her mother to death. Father and daughter act out mutual incestuous desires in *The Crazies*. Both films open with the break-down of the family. How do you feel about this breakdown?

GR: I just think that it has been breaking down. We don't seem to have the same sort of respect for the family as before. It just seems to be a functional thing not having the same mystical awareness it used to have and does not seem to be providing anything directive for people's lives. In fact they're spending all their time figuring how to escape all those responsibilities in terms of ties, for good or bad.

RW: What is striking is the total lack of family nostalgia at all.

GR: At the end of *Dawn*, Fran who's pregnant flies off with a black man. That's the potential of a new kind of family. I don't have any nostalgia for the traditional family, only for individuals. The family is no longer an operative part of our lives.

RW: This raises the question of social change and the film maker's responsibility to it. Brian de Palma said that society was impossible, there's no possibility of changing it, and all you can do is enjoy the corruption. What he said is fascinating. He adopts a kind of metaphysical stance saying, more or less, that we will die so what's the point? Stephanie Rothman and Wes Craven both expressed much more positively committed ideas, or at least an intervention in influencing society for cultural progress and change. How do you stand in relation to these ideas?

GR: I get my information from what goes on around me in terms of the attitudes which go into my films; probably more than the topics themselves. In places such as Harlem, to start thinking about positive action in building themselves as positive members of society. Frankly, in capitalistic societies the answer has been to give people something to work for. I suppose, if you gave them $3–4,000,000 for them to build themselves up something would happen. But I think that pretty soon it would grow and develop into what we have now. The focus has not been on human development. The issue for me is not "Are we going down the road to the Apocalypse?" We don't attempt to understand. We go along the way that society goes. It's difficult to see changes in ourselves and even more for the public to see what they've become part of. I think I understand what Brian says: but there are aspects of it that you can't possibly enjoy. I can understand something like the punk of sleaze movement when there's nothing left but McDonalds! I can have fun with that but I can't possibly enjoy what's happening to society. It's very easy to blame government or corporations or anything else but it's really our own responsibility. We must make decisions for ourselves. I'm not going to be a part of this or that. But since film is a creative medium, film's business aspect tends to intensify those things that people don't feel particularly comfortable with in terms of tackiness. The film business is a particularly nebulous kind of business with intangibles where everything is renegotiable and an inherent lack of morality which seems to pervade the business side. The whole atmosphere is of some degree of corruption and lack of substance.

RW: *Dawn* seems to set up two traditional symbols of male authority—the gun and the helicopter. At the end the man surrenders the gun and the woman pilots the copter. They fly off on equal terms, perhaps set up a new cooperative society as Stephanie Rothman and Wes Craven envisage for their films.

GR: Yes. That would be intentional. Fran is not a traditional horror movie woman. It's not true. She's always correct. She does finally step up and compete, perhaps misguidedly, with the men when she straps on the guns. But after the hunt she walks away disgusted realizing that's not what it's about. She is a natural victim. She gets left behind because she's pregnant but I don't think that's sexist. It's meant to reflect what actually happens. Fran does become an effective character.

Tony Williams: Why another living dead movie?
GR: When I was making *Night of the Living Dead* I had no idea that I would make another film like it so I resisted it for a long time. It's not another sequel in the usual sense. There's a complex set of reasons. But I originally wrote it as a trilogy at three different stages of the phenomenon. It really was talking about revolution and does have to go to that extreme case where the revolutionary society is operative but nothing is changed. So I got comfortable with that. Originally I wrote the story with all three parts, happening in the same little farmhouse. When I finally got resigned to making the second film I wanted it to be its own film. The attitude is completely different. It grows out of what is happening today rather than what was happening in 1968. So there seemed to be good enough reasons to go ahead and do it.

TW: Where did you find the supermarket? It seems such an ideal location.
GR: I knew the supermarket was there. I knew the people who owned it, and that's where I got the idea to write the script. I was playing around with the ideas in my head and I went out on a tour with the owners who happened to be friends. I wrote a script, changed it. The people let us go in and shoot. It would have been very hard to get that sort of cooperation. So we began in November 1977.

TW: Was the deal with Dario Argento set up beforehand?
GR: Oh, yes. It was a long time putting the deal together because it was a bigger budget than we'd ever had. The deal with Dario enabled it to happen. He and I talked about doing some other things, trying to get some other independent directors involved because even if you've had some moderate successes it's very hard to get some money together. Because of Dario lending his business credentials, we were able to put a deal together making money in both territories.

TW: You used unknown actors again?
GR: Ken Foree has done some American TV such as *Kojak* and he was in one feature film called *Bingo Long*. He was in New York's Black Theatre. I

didn't know him before I met him at a casting session. David Emge is a Pittsburgher. He was teaching for a couple of years and I always wanted to use him. Scotty is an old friend of ours, working here at a restaurant where we hang out and has done some off-Broadway theatre. Gaylen just came out of a casting session. They're all now trying to get work. No one has yet. Scotty has a bit part in *The Wanderers*. David's doing theatre. He's the only one who didn't try to go to Hollywood. He stayed East Coast.

TW: *Night of the Living Dead* also used Pittsburgh people.
GR: Yes. Duane Jones (Ben) was a friend of ours for six years. He was living in New York at the time and came back to do it. Judith O'Dea (Barbara) returned after doing vocational theatre on the West Coast. All the principals are vocational except Judith Ridley (the girl blown up in the truck). Most of the people in secondary roles in *The Crazies* have been people from summer stock theatre in Pennsylvania.

RW: You don't use stars in your films nor have you built up a kind of stock company like Robert Altman.
GR: Yes. There are some actors who turn up in two of the films but I haven't seen a reason to build up that kind of company per se. I can't imagine it would be a necessary thing to do at all. On the production side we do have that kind of nuclear system.

RW: John Amplas who plays Martin is credited as casting director on *Dawn*. But why the lack of stars?
GR: I don't have any explicit objection to using a name if they're right for a role and available for the budgeting reasons.

RW: What about the seeming paradox about the statements you attempt in your films and the majority audience's wish to see violence?
GR: Unfortunately I think 80 percent of the audience goes to see the violence. That's really what *Dawn* satirizes on the surface. There's nothing really you can do but react to it and begin to question yourself. But no audience is the same. The New York one reacted like an old-fashioned movie audience.

RL: But it's more of a catharsis than in *Martin*. To see a shopping mall smashed up is more of an exhilaration.

RR: At first the Ontario censor refused it totally so we had to tell them, "It's not supposed to be taken seriously." They said, "Oh?" It's so highly stylized and exaggerated as to be absurd black comedy.

RW: In Wes Craven's films, *The Last House on the Left* and *The Hills Have Eyes*, the violence is so disturbing that it's impossible to enjoy. Everybody enjoys the violence in *Dawn*. Do you see this as a moral problem?

GR: If you watch the battles in Errol Flynn's *San Antonio* which go on for forty-five minutes you see it's exactly the same kind of thing. You become conditioned to watch that kind of violence where the good guys fight the bad guys but in *Dawn* I haven't defined who is good or bad. That's something you think about when you go out. I was going for that pop culture splatter look. You can buy artificial blood but it looks artificial so you have to get Tom Savini to work on it for several days to make it look good, but with *Dawn* I left it alone. Playing it out to its absolute extreme is what softens it.

RW: Roger's crypto-Fascist glee in the hunt scenes receives critical treatment but at the same time the film plays on our enjoyment of the violence. The audience's reaction is never criticized.

GR: But in certain senses I say that the film is a pie in the audience's face. It satirizes that kind of audience.

Q: Do you see yourself as having an influence on the horror genre or any films in particular?

GR: I don't know. I would hope that what we do will ultimately influence independent cinema in the States. We have insisted on staying smaller rather than going on to the lot. Dario said, "Look, we'll give you office space." But although we'd be independent producers we'd be "beholden." One of the things that we tried to do is really talk and communicate as much as possible about the business side. There's no organization for independent producers. We need some form of mainstream distribution to reach the audience. It's very hard for me to think whether I have an influence on the genre, the media etc. since what I try to do is get to know the business and help people out.

TW: Generally, in your films the music soundtrack plays a very functional role. But in *Dawn* you used Goblin who scored the operatic horror movie *Suspiria*.

GR: Goblin link with Dario, unfortunately, because I'm very concerned about my track record. In fact when I cut a film, I don't cut on a Steenbeck but on a tape deck because there's something about the functioning of the individual elements that I like. I usually cut on 16mm even if we shoot on 35. It's easier to handle, I can see what's happening. I cut double tracks at the same time for economic reasons. I believe that people don't get a chance to develop a lot of experience with the total medium. Nowadays in Hollywood and TV other people cut picture and visuals then send it elsewhere for sound effects. I'm actively involved with all these elements even when I'm making my first cut. I like to see all those mixed so that's why we keep those small facilities in our Pittsburgh shop so I can see, even on a rough cut, all those elements working against each other because I use a lot of complex tracks.

Music, to me, is one of the tools we can use to manipulate. I don't mean to say that I'm not trying to manipulate the audience because on the surface presentation that's at least what the film is trying to do, what Brian de Palma calls "grammar." To translate to the audience all those are tools. Not many people look at the juxtaposition of frame to frame but music. It was unfortunate that I didn't have a lot of chances to really integrate those Goblin tracks. I used a lot of very traditional songs and funky stuff like the Muzak. Goblin were doing one third track simultaneously and the tracks on our version are a little bit harder because I like a lot of their music. Dario's version on his European score has a lot more Goblin. But he went the other way. He tried to do that *Suspiria* experience. But we didn't really have the film to fit into that. Neither version is exactly what it should be. But I was trying to bring it close so I used some other kind of library music that bridged between Goblin and the other traditional stuff.

RR: It had to do with the quality because when we got it into the picture George had to set in a scratch track. When Goblin went to compose their original score they parodied most of what George had given indications of. In the Italian version instead of actual Muzak you hear a similar high fidelity sound.

GR: The Nagra had a different score so they just redid it in quadrophenia. Some of those things didn't work on their version.

Q: Which direction do you see your third film going?

GR: I don't know. That's why I'd like to spend a little time and see where we all go.

Knight after Night with George Romero

Dan Yakir/1981

From *American Film*, May 1981, 42–45, 69. © 1981 American Film Institute. Reprinted by permission.

During the past thirteen years, filmgoers have come to associate George Romero's name with gore and violence. Through such horror classics as *Night of the Living Dead* and, more recently, *Dawn of the Dead*, he has not only acquired a large cult following but has become—alongside John Carpenter—the most successful independent filmmaker ever. Budgeted at $114,000, *Night of the Living Dead* grossed $20 million, and the $1.5 million *Dawn of the Dead* made more than $55 million. The figures speak for themselves, but Romero, whose early pictures met with snickering, often hostile reviews, has also won growing critical recognition as a filmmaker with a subversive, original vision.

His latest—and most ambitious—project is *Knightriders*. Just released, it's hardly the kind of movie one might expect from the creator of the screen's first cannibalistic zombies. "It's about an eclectic group of people who establish their own lifestyle, apart from society," the affable forty-one-year-old director explains. "They live by a medieval code of ethics—chivalry, morality. In essence, it's a traveling Renaissance fair whose main attraction is a jousting tournament, medieval style—on motorcycles."

Romero quickly adds, "They're athletes, not Hell's Angels—and they have a great act. But after two years on the road, the attention of the media makes it hard for them to maintain their code of ethics. Lust and greed pull them in different directions, but they finally realize they can't go back to society. What started as an on-the-road survival tactic has become their own world: Through the code, they have rediscovered their conscience."

While Romero terms the film "an action-adventure romance with an edge of fantasy," he says he is aware that "the industry might define

69

it as a bike movie." With a smile he declares, "Well, it is and it isn't. *Knightriders* borrows much more from *Ivanhoe* than from the movies of Hal Needham or Roger Corman. It's at once more intimate—and a lot bigger—than my other films, and we get to know the characters better than in my previous work." The two central characters are Billy (Ed Harris), the "king" of the group, who manages, in Romero's words, to "live on another plane, on an absolute plateau," and Merlin (played by black actor Brother Blue), who "does what he likes best—scat around and pull Arthurian stories from his back pocket."

As the name suggests, *Knightriders* leans heavily on the Arthurian myth—in the relationships among the characters (there's even a replay of the Lancelot-Guinevere-Arthur triangle) and in the importance of ceremony and ritual in the group's life. Romero acknowledges that the film is casting a nostalgic glance toward the past. It's only there, he believes, that the desire for social order and the quest for self-realization find fulfillment.

These concerns turn up repeatedly in Romero's previous films: in *It's Always Vanilla,* which he considers a cross between *The Graduate* and *Goodbye, Columbus*; in *Jack's Wife,* about marriage and the evils of suburban life; in *The Crazies,* an "antimilitary" film set against the backdrop of a nuclear disaster; and in *Martin,* a modern vampire story.

Despite the grimness of pictures like *Night of the Living Dead* and *Dawn of the Dead,* Romero insists that his own view of life is optimistic. "If there's anything that bothers me," he says, "it's when I read that *Night* has spawned the new wave of horror films, because I don't consider it inhuman at all. Even *Dawn* is not *mean*. It's not about how rotten we are." Romero says he decided to make *Knightriders* in part to tell people "they still had a chance." After all, he points out, "the underbelly in all my movies is the longing for a better world, for a higher plane of existence, for people to get together. I'm still singing these songs."

But Romero says he knows that messages do not sell films. They have to be sugarcoated within a genre framework. Not that he finds that is a high price to pay. "I love working with genre. I loved all genre movies when I was a kid, and I still want to make a jungle movie—*Tarzan!*—a war movie, and a Western."

"I always wanted to make a knights movie," Romero says, and five years ago he approached American International Pictures (now Filmways) with a proposal for "a real medieval period picture." The response was negative. The disheartened Romero told Sam Arkoff, then

AIP's chairman, "Maybe I should put the knights on motorcycles and add a rock 'n' roll sound track. Then you'll jack it up!" But this outburst planted the bike idea in his own mind, and when he discovered the Society for Creative Anachronisms—a group that celebrates the medieval experience "pretty much the way our group does in the film"—the script practically wrote itself.

"*Knightriders* is meant to be a commercial picture," Romero says, "which is why we have stunts. But they don't overpower the film. They're in their place, the way the jousting sequences in *Ivanhoe* or *Camelot* were in theirs." The stunts, performed by many of Hal Needham's regulars, are spectacular. "Instead of shooting them in slow motion," says Romero, cinematographer Michael Gornick "risked his life by getting so close to the jousts he practically became a part of them half the time."

Romero himself is a filmmaker who gets totally involved with his projects—from preproduction to the editing and looping stage. He insists on doing himself what another director would relegate to a second unit.

Romero's passion for moviemaking is contagious. "I started as a boom man in the sound department on the set of *The Crazies*," remembers Michael Gornick, "and I stayed on—because of George. I couldn't believe filmmaking was like this: It was so enjoyable. There was an absolute free form in that shop then, as there is now. Because of this atmosphere and George's attitude toward people and talent, you could make progress. Within one year, I was shooting and cutting. While in the industry you have a narrow specialty and move slowly forward, I experimented in all departments until I found what I wanted to do."

Knightriders is Romero's first union production, and the small, close-knit crew he used to work with grew to two hundred. "But it worked fine," Romero says. "I like to create an environment where people can contribute to the film. In most cases, actors and technicians are simply told what to do. I like to be approachable and have an open dialogue among all." Partly to preserve the informal atmosphere he cherishes, Romero has so far avoided working with name actors. The atmosphere, he fears, might prove too fragile to sustain inflated egos and capricious temperaments. "My producer, Richard Rubinstein, always says, 'You shouldn't hold it against them that they have a name!' And I don't have an implicit objection to working with stars, but they have to be right for the part and fit in. So far, there is no need." By now, he has cultivated a troupe of regulars, some of whom first came to the set as curious high school students. They simply never left. "They loved movies—and in Pittsburgh, this was the only game in town."

Romero's own love for the movies grew out of his lonely childhood in the Bronx, where he created, he says, "my own fantasy world" with the aid of EC comic books and B-movies. At fourteen, he made "The Man from the Meteor" with an 8mm movie camera borrowed from his uncle. One scene involved throwing a dummy in flames from a roof, for which the young George was picked up by the police.

He left home to study painting, design, and drama at the Carnegie-Mellon Institute in Pittsburgh and, in 1962, formed a company that soon evolved into Pittsburgh's top producer of television commercials, documentaries, and industrial films. The next step was joining with ten partners, each investing $600, to buy film and rent the farmhouse that became the set of *Night of the Living Dead*.

Romero has continued to work out of Pittsburgh, allowing him to maintain his independence from industry pressures and influences. *Knightriders*, which cost $3.7 million, "is the first big production that's been locally spawned," he points out. "Everybody feels, Hey, we've finally made a *real* movie!"

Tiny by industry standards, the budget was footed by United Film Distribution, which released *Dawn of the Dead* nationally, and United Artists, which acquired *Dawn* for some overseas territories. It's the first time that Romero's company, Laurel Entertainment, Inc., has obtained major studio backing. He says there were no strings attached—he had full creative control, including final cut. The movie industry, Romero asserts, "is a power-oriented business that uses talent as a commodity. If I had made a deal with a studio at any point in my career up to now, all I would get offered would be a little horror picture. There's no reason to involve twenty other people in the process if you can do it on your own. And that's what I did."

Romero does it on his own—in partnership with Richard Rubinstein, who is based in New York. "He's an excellent business partner who gets deals made—with the controls I want. He doesn't interfere in my work, and I don't covet his job. It's perfect. But I'm still in no position to dictate something—I still have a drawer full of scripts I'd like to make one day. If you want to keep operating in this business, you have to find the path of least resistance. I feel I still haven't done *exactly* what I wanted."

Romero's cost consciousness is evident in the way he works. ("I respect that here's only so much money and I'm not going to have a crew sitting around for the sun to appear through the trees," he has said.) Shots, he says, are set up rapidly. "What we've developed as a working style is banging through it—that's where you get the other side of that cinema energy. If we spend the morning doing one shot and the afternoon another, we'd have to use a big master shot, which I don't do. I don't think a studio production could achieve the same effect *Knightriders* has without a six-month shoot. We took half as long."

Romero's upcoming projects include two written by the best-selling novelist Stephen King, who makes a brief appearance in *Knightriders* as a beer-guzzling hillbilly. They are *Creepshow*, a collection of horror tales told in a comic book style, which starts shooting in June, and *The Stand*, based on King's novel. "I usually write my own material," says Romero, "but for once, it'll be nice to just have it handed to me."

The two met when Warner Bros. approached Romero to direct *'Salem's Lot*, another King novel. But because of the escalating costs of several rewrites, the film rights were sold to television and *'Salem's Lot* was shot by Tobe Hooper. Although Romero likes Hooper's film and also sees much to praise in Brian De Palma's *Carrie*, both "were off." King, says Romero, "has been very frustrated about all these experiences—and we hope to do it right. I like the humanity in his work, which is really a part of the genre and goes back to *Nosferatu, Frankenstein,* and *The Cabinet of Dr. Caligari*. It's always there in Steve's work, no matter how gruesome the surface is. That's precisely what was missing from *The Shining*—there were no real people in Kubrick's film."

Unlike *Creepshow, The Stand* is an expensive project which is likely to require star casting and, in Romero's words, "various ancillary values." But both King and Romero agree that unless they can do it their way, they won't do it at all. Other projects? There is *Invasion of the Spaghetti Monsters*, a UFO farce "with little green men and the first real flying saucer landing. We might even go for a few cameos—John Agar, Faith Domergue." And finally there is *Day of the Dead*, the third and last part of the zombie saga. A production deal exists, but Romero made sure the film wouldn't have to be shot in the next four years. He is simply too busy, even for zombies.

George Romero:
Revealing the Monsters within Us

Tom Seligson/1981

From *Rod Serling's The Twilight Zone Magazine*, August 1981, 12–17. Reprinted by permission.

With his first film, *Night of the Living Dead* (1968), director George Romero made a spectacular debut. Shot for a mere $70,000 with a cast of Pittsburgh unknowns, the film did for zombies what *Jaws* later did for sharks. It soon became a horror cult classic, grossed over $10 million, and introduced Romero as a master of the horror genre.

Many young directors would have caught the next plane to Hollywood, but Romero is a maverick. Remaining in Pittsburgh and worried about being typed as a horror director, he followed up *Night* with *It's Always Vanilla* (1970) and *Jack's Wife* (1971), two films that were not widely distributed and did little for his career. Still, he kept working, churning out commercials, sports specials for television, and a politically oriented sf feature called *The Crazies* (1972).

It was his return to the horror genre in *Martin* (1977) that drew renewed critical attention to this staunchly independent filmmaker whom *Newsweek* hailed as "a dazzling stylist" whose "balance of wit and horror is the best since Hitchcock." Then came *Dawn of the Dead* (1979), a sequel to *Night*, which *Rolling Stone* picked as the number-one film of the year and which has grossed $55 million to date.

Romero's latest film, *Knightriders*, is about modern-day knights who joust on motorcycles, and what it lacks in horror it makes up for in spectacle. Future films include the film version of Stephen King's *The Stand*; *Creepshow*, based on King's first original screenplay; and *Day of the Dead*, the third film in Romero's zombie trilogy.

Romero is forty-one, married to the actress Christine Forrest (who has appeared in most of his films), and continues to live in Pittsburgh. He's a hulking man whose size would frighten you on a deserted street—that is, until you saw his face. With his gray flecked beard, soft blue eyes, and dimples, this master of horror couldn't scare a pussycat.

TZ: You've been making movies ever since you were young. Were you always interested in horror films?

Romero: I loved all genre films—horror movies as well as war pictures and cowboy films. Whenever one was at a neighborhood theater or on television, I'd watch it. That's the way I learned how they worked. However, it was just circumstance, the fact that *Night of the Living Dead* was my first picture, that I got a reputation as a director of horror films. I chose the genre because I liked it, and because I wanted to do something commercial.

TZ: *Night of the Living Dead* has come to be considered a classic independent film. How did you make it for so little money?

Romero: First of all, it was based on a short story that I wrote. I didn't have to buy the rights. Then a friend of mine and I collaborated on the screenplay. The production was also very simple. At the time, I had a small film company going. We were doing commercials primarily, but we had all the hardware and a crew of people, and that's what we used to make the film. Plus we used a lot of friends in the cast—even some of the advertising people we were working with in Pittsburgh. They came out to play the zombies. There was a great deal of local cooperation, because we were the first feature film based out of Pittsburgh.

TZ: Were the actors professional?

Romero: Three or four of them were. But as professional as you can get as an actor in Pittsburgh means doing radio or television. Primarily the cast was friends and people who showed up.

TZ: I've heard you were unable to get a major studio to distribute the film. Why do you think you had so much trouble?

Romero: Well, for one thing, I really didn't know what I was doing. After I made the film, I literally threw it in the trunk of the car and brought it to New York. The first studio I called was Columbia, and I was surprised when they told me to come on in with the film. They held it for three months. They kept saying, "It's great" and "We're thinking about it." But finally they turned it down, because the film was in black and white, and it was hard to get drive-ins to play black and white pictures.

The next studio I went to was AIP. They said, "Change the ending, and you've got a deal."

TZ: How did they want it changed?
Romero: They didn't want the hero to die. But I refused to do it. It would have changed what the picture was about. By this time, five months had gone by, and I decided to forget the major studios and get my own sales rep. Finally the Walter Reade-Continental chain made an offer, and I took it.

TZ: Were you surprised when *Night of the Living Dead* became such a success on the midnight cult circuit?
Romero: Very much—although that was in its second wave. The film was an immediate hit on the drive-in circuit. That's what a lot of people don't realize. It made a lot of money right away. In fact, the only money that it ever returned to us was during that first nine months. After that, the film sort of dropped out of existence for about a year and a half. Then Walter Reade released it on a double bill with a film called *Slaves*. Rex Reed and some of the other critics wrote that it was better than *Slaves*. Then the Elgin and the Waverly and a couple of other theaters started to play it at midnight. It began to get international press, and that really surprised me. I knew that it was a good horror film, but by this point, all I could see in it were the flaws, the things I wished I could go back and correct.

TZ: Despite your own dissatisfaction, the film's success was certainly important to your career.
Romero: Yes and no. I was able to raise the money right away to make more movies. But in retrospect, I think it happened too quickly. Though I did have ideas for other films, I had no idea what the business was about. I was just a guy making beer commercials in Pittsburgh.

TZ: I've read that you were reluctant to do another horror picture right away, for fear you'd be typed as a horror director.
Romero: That's true. So what did I do? I went and made two films that probably six people saw—*It's Always Vanilla* and *Jack's Wife*. I learned a lot from them in terms of developing as a filmmaker, but what they

really taught me was the nature of the film business. I learned that the film industry is not going to accept serious little dramas from some up-start in Pittsburgh—especially if the films have no stars. As they say in the biz, there's no bottom-side protection. Those two films taught me what the odds were against that kind of small personal film. I still don't think those films are bad, I just think they were the wrong kind of film to make at that stage in my career.

TZ: Is that why you returned to the horror genre?

Romero: No, because I didn't—at least not right away. After those two films, I got involved with a small independent New York distributor, Cambist, and I made *The Crazies*. It's a disaster film about a bio-weapons spill. This film didn't hit, either, but in this case the problem was not with the film, but with the handling. When the distributor saw the rough cut, he thought he had *Jaws* on his hands. Consequently he tried to open it too big, and he spent a lot of money just opening in New York. It was a lot of money for him, but it wasn't enough to compete with the big studios. He ended up having to shelve the film.

TZ: Tell me more about the film itself.

Romero: It was inspired by the science fiction disaster films of the 1950s. It's about a plane that crashes, spilling a substance designed for germ warfare. Nobody knows exactly what's going on. People are being affected by the germ, but they don't know it. All they know is that the army has come into town and is trying to herd them all together. The soldiers are just as confused as the townspeople. There are only a few officials in the Pentagon who know what actually happened, and what results is a conflict between the townspeople and the military forces.

TZ: It sounds very political.

Romero: It is. It was made just around the time of Kent State. You remember how angry people were about the shootings on the campus by the National Guard. Ultimately, I think, the film deals with the politics a little too lightly. It has sort of an outrageous, bawdy style, and some people may have thought we were making fun of politics, exploiting Vietnam and the Kent State tragedy. We weren't at all. In fact, *The Crazies* was a very angry and radical film, if one sees through the comic surface.

TZ: Who are the Crazies in the title? The soldiers or the townspeople?

Romero: The people. Once they come in contact with the bug, they go crazy. However, there's a scientist brought in to handle the situation who observes that you can't tell who's crazy and who's not.

TZ: It sounds to some extent like what happens in *Night of the Living Dead*, in which the people who are alive get killed and almost immediately turn into zombies.

Romero: That's because I was dealing with the same idea in both movies—how easily the victim becomes the monster. For instance, in *Night of the Living Dead*, take those scenes with the little girl. Her mother's trying to protect her, but then the girl dies, and seconds later she's a zombie, going after her mother. What I'm trying to show is how the monster, the evil, is not something lurking in the distance, but something actually inside all of us.

That's what Stephen King shows so well. He takes a real situation, a very mundane situation, and throws it just two degrees out of whack. It's like *Village of the Damned*, where those delightful little children are really the evil ones. That's a very scary thing. It's like meeting an insane person on the street.

TZ: Talking about what constitutes horror, the next big feature you did was *Martin*. I remember the *Newsweek* review, which said, "Romero poses the question of whether the hero, Martin, is in fact an eighty-four-year-old vampire from Transylvania or an eighteen-year-old psychotic from Pittsburgh." Is that how you saw the movie?

Romero: In a way. *Martin* is designed to show that all those supernatural monsters that are part of our literary tradition are, in essence, expurgations of ourselves. They are beasts we've created in order to exorcise the monster from within us. Whether it's a monster made out of spare parts, one that grows out of us, or something we turn into during a full moon, monsters have traditionally been considered embodiments of our own evil. By distinguishing them from us, we could destroy them. I tried to show in *Martin* that you can't just slice off this evil part of ourselves and throw it away. It's a permanent part of us, and we'd better try to understand it.

TZ: Are you saying that we're all innately evil?

Romero: "Potentially evil" is a better way of putting it. I don't think there's an intrinsically evil side to man. But I think all of us at certain times in our lives do things that are compromising, things that go against our conscience. There's a line we won't cross, and for all of us it's a question of "Where is that line?" Sometimes we stretch it a bit. No matter who we are, and how much we're satisfied with our own behavior, there are always those moments we feel guilty about. That's the guilt we're trying to unload by creating monsters. We can then punish ourselves by punishing the monster, allowing our good side to prevail. In *Martin*, by showing an eighteen-year-old psychotic kid who on one hand is himself and on the other hand is this monster, I'm showing that the monster can never die. It's like in *Night of the Living Dead*. You can kill the monster, but your next-door neighbor may become him tomorrow.

TZ: In real life, who would you be more afraid to run into on a dark Pittsburgh street—the vampire or the young psychotic?

Romero: Probably the psychotic, because he looks normal, but a second later he could change. That's precisely the point I'm trying to make. Traditionally, whenever we see vampires in the movies, we've come to expect a certain predictable behavior. For example, we all know that vampires are only going to frighten us at night, and that to get rid of them, all we have to do is find their casket and put a stake through their heart. What I'm trying to show in *Martin* is that we can't expect the monster to be predictable. That's also what Steve's saying in his books.

TZ: One of the things I found most interesting about *Martin*, and which lends itself to what you're saying, is the fact that he uses razors against his victims, rather than fangs. I think that makes him much more horrifying.

Romero: Visually it's certainly more horrifying. It also makes him more mysterious. Fangs don't come out just when he feels the need, and the need is not connected to the moon or the night. However, on the other hand, Martin's got a very detailed and meticulous M.O. He uses syringes and razor blades. He has a little kit with breaking and entering tools, and he knows about things like burglar alarms, and electric garage-door openers, which is one of those supposedly fail-safe devices, but which he uses to get into the one house he attacks. That's another level of *Martin*. It's saying that the very things we take comfort in and feel safe because we have, like garage-door openers, are in fact not going to save us.

TZ: In the case of *Martin*, did you have the different levels of the film thought out in advance, or did they just develop?

Romero: I planned it all in advance. I always do that. It's a self-preservation technique. Knowing what this business is like, I don't like to sit down and do a final script and get all excited and emotionally involved with it until I know for sure there's a deal. And thanks to the talents of my partner, I've been in the luxurious position of making all of our deals on the basis of treatments and story ideas. Consequently, all of the films I've made come from ideas that I've had for a year or more. I have little index files with story-line ideas, and I work on them a lot. But it's not until I know the film's definitely going to be made that I actually sit down and write the final script. I think it's important to be in touch with the story at the time you're doing it. I would hate to take out one of my old scripts that's been sitting in the drawer and film it without being able to rework it.

TZ: As a novelist, I know that when you're in the process of writing scenes that are particularly horrifying, they can sometimes have a chilling effect. Does the same thing happen to you as a director? Or because it's a group enterprise, with so many people around, does that diminish the thrill?

Romero: It happens when you're cutting the film. It's four in the morning, you're all alone working on a scene, and you finish it, shut off the lights, and play it for yourself. Those are the times one of your own scenes may frighten you. It's happened to me three or four times. It happened with *Night of the Living Dead*, with a couple of scenes in *Martin*, and with the knitting needle scene in *The Crazies*. It's a scene with a little old lady—again, it's one of those things that are two degrees off-whack. She's sitting in a rocking chair, knitting. A soldier walks in to take her to safety, and she lays into him with her knitting needle. That scene really got to me the first time I saw it.

TZ: What about when you rescreen one of your movies? Does it still have an effect on you, or have you seen it too often?

Romero: I make a habit of laying off my films for long periods of time, and then taking a fresh look. After it was first made, I laid off *Night of the Living Dead* for three years. Even when I would be speaking about it somewhere, I wouldn't sit in while it was being shown. That's because all I could see were the problems. Right now, I haven't seen the film for four years.

Even when you're making the film, it's sometimes hard to tell whether it's working. In that respect, filmmaking is different from writing. I know that when I write a script, I can lay off it for a few days and then go back and get a sense of how it's reading. A film is different when you're working on it, because you see it over and over. You see how the images cut against each other, and you know exactly what's coming. You really need time away from it before you can let it affect your senses with any degree of freshness.

The impact of film is basically visceral—and that's particularly so, with horror, as well as comedy. Whenever you're trying to evoke a spontaneous reaction, like a laugh, a cry, or a startle, it's a very delicate process. You don't know if it's working, because you yourself never get to experience it for the first time. It's really instrument flying. You're banking on understanding intellectually that if you connect this sound with this image, then you'll get a rise out of the audience.

TZ: But you don't really know until you show it to people?
Romero: That's right. And sometimes it's a very rude awakening. The first time you have it is in front of forty people. If everyone sits there and the suspense or horror doesn't hit them, you know it's not working. You can just feel it.

TZ: Do you make a point of seeing the films of other horror directors?
Romero: Sure. I go to see everyone else's work. I like John Carpenter a lot. He's really very skilled at frightening you, and I think *Halloween* is beautiful. I also think David Cronenberg does a good job. I like both *The Brood* and *Scanners*. Another favorite director of mine is Roman Polanski. I thought *Repulsion* was incredible, especially the scene with the mirror. Catherine Deneuve opens a door that has a mirror on it, and as the door is moving, there's maybe a frame or two where you see, in the mirror, a figure standing behind her. There's not even a sound, but it's a real heart-stopper. The film itself is beautifully crafted. It tightens all your nerve endings and makes you ready for something horrifying.

Alien did that, too. *Alien* is an example of how a film can create tension regardless of its story. If you really think about it, we've seen that kind of plot, before. What gives the film its tension is the sight of those empty halls, plus the steam and the noise, all of which has a very visceral impact. It wasn't the jumps that were particularly effective.

TZ: What do you mean by jumps?

Romero: Jumps are when you manipulate the audience into literally jumping in their seats. Anybody can do them. You can make an audience jump with ninety minutes of black leader in which, at random intervals, you've put a white frame synchronized with a loud noise. That'll make them jump. Of course, it's not the same thing as really putting the audience on edge and holding them there.

TZ: What do you think of the many cheapie horror pictures that have recently come out? Films like *Terror Train* and *Maniac* and *Motel Hell?*
Romero: A lot of these films are made simply because there's a wave going on. They're being made in Buffalo, North Carolina, everywhere. That happens anytime there's a trend that's within the reach of small independent filmmakers. I don't think many of them are any good. They don't have much integrity, or even an affection for the genre. They're just deals.

Motel Hell was one of the more interesting of the bunch. It was actually very funny. Rory Calhoun plays this innkeeper-butcher who turns his guests into pork sausage. It was intended to be a send-up of horror pictures. The problem was they tried to play it both ways, as horror and comedy.

TZ: Is that possible to do?
Romero: It's hard, but I think there's room for it. If you watch a fifties horror movie now, you'll laugh all the way through—even at *The Thing*. It's hilarious. I tried to play it both ways with *Dawn of the Dead.*

TZ: I can see that. A lot of critics have commented on how the film is more than just a horror film; because it takes place in a shopping mall, it's also seen as a satire on American consumerism. Was that your intention from the start?
Romero: *Dawn of the Dead* is the second part of an intended trilogy, all of which is based on my original short story. In the story, everything occurs in the farmhouse. Different groups of people show up at different times. When I started to make *Dawn*, I decided to change that. The phenomenon of the zombies is continuing—it's expanding, in fact—so I decided that I didn't want to keep it at the same location. I also wanted to change the texture of the sequel, to make it bawdier. I once said *Night of the Living Dead* was a fifties film made in the sixties. Well, *Dawn* is a sixties film made in the seventies. And maybe the third one will be a seventies film made in the eighties.

In *Dawn of the Dead*, I wanted a surface texture that would provide for small confined spaces while also reflecting on what America is becoming—a sterile, fast-food society. At first I wasn't sure how to convey that idea. But I happen to know the people who own the mall. I was out there one day taking a tour of it, and suddenly I realized that I had to do it there. I sat down and wrote an original treatment, played with it a bit, and finally did the script. By then we had a deal to do the film, and so I was able to write it with the mall in mind.

TZ: I gather the owners gave you complete cooperation.
Romero: Totally. And so did the individual merchants. The only ones we had some difficulty with were the chains, and that's only because they had to get approval from headquarters.

TZ: Has that mall become famous as a result of the film? Is there a plaque out front—or better yet, a statue of a zombie?
Romero: I'm afraid not! But I'll tell you this, the film certainly hasn't hurt business any. Not that anything could.

TZ: Where do you go in the third part of the trilogy? I've heard it's called *Day of the Dead*.
Romero: That's just a working title. I don't know what we'll eventually call it. As far as the story is concerned, the film deals with a time when the zombies appear to have become the new society. But then we begin to wonder: If there aren't any more people, how are they eating? Then we find out that, in fact, there are more people, and that the zombies are being fed—something I alluded to in *Dawn of the Dead*. Finally we come to realize that their food supply is being farmed. The story progresses from there. I don't want to say much more than that.

TZ: That's intriguing enough! When's the film going to be made?
Romero: Contractually we don't have to do it for five years. I wanted some time in between. Maybe it's an ego thing, but I feel really gratified that the two films have become as well known as they are. I also like the idea that they reflect two different eras in terms of when they were made. I would really like it if the third film in the series could reflect still another period. I admit that it might be very indulgent and egotistical to wait like this, but I'm going to do it anyway.

TZ: This brings me to your latest picture, *Knightriders*, which is not a horror picture. How did you come to make it?

Romero: Several years ago I was in a meeting with Sam Arkoff, who was the head of AIP. I told him that I wanted to do a spaghetti King Arthur movie, set in the period. I wanted to show the knights the way they really were: infected and syphilitic and so forth. Sam said, "No, you'd be killing a legend. Also, no one wants to see that medieval stuff now." So I said, sort of facetiously, "Well, how about putting the knights on motorcycles and using rock and roll?" Sam said, "That's not a bad idea. You may have something there."

I thought about it several weeks later, and subsequently went back in to see the studios with a concept that was very close to what *Knightriders* is now. But they always read it as a kind of *Death Race 2000* or a bike picture. I think that, until they actually saw it, even the distributors of the film and the people who financed the production thought of it more as a bike film than what it is—namely, a film of modern-day knights trying to live out the King Arthur legend.

TZ: What interested you about the King Arthur legend in the first place?

Romero: Again, it was old genre movies. I'd give my eyeteeth to make an *Ivanhoe*. In *Knightriders*, I'm borrowing from two different genres. I'm borrowing from all those Cornel Wilde, Robert Taylor movies. And I'm also borrowing from the great American bike movie.

Basically, it's a film about idealism. It's about a group of people who are trying to live their own lifestyle completely separate and apart from the rest of society. They are all members of a traveling Renaissance fair. They travel from town to town, holding jousting tournaments on motorcycles. Instead of searching for the Holy Grail, their quest is to keep themselves uncorrupted, despite the media's attempt to commercialize them.

TZ: *Knightriders*, of course, is not the only current picture about medieval legend. There's *Excalibur*, which is set in the period, and *Dragonslayer*, a sword and sorcery picture, and several others not yet in production. Why this sudden interest in the medieval era? Are we reaching back to something more glamorous?

Romero: Definitely. I think there's a longing for romance again. We've been trying to create a kind of romance out of things that aren't romantic, and I think we're finally realizing it. We haven't had romance in our music for a hell of a long time—not since the Beatles. There's also a longing for a certain kind of morality again, a personal sense of honor and conscience. That's what *Knightriders* is about—about people trying to live by their own simple code, independent of the rest of society.

TZ: I know that the budget on this picture was about $4 million, which is roughly three times what *Dawn* cost. Was directing the picture a more anxious experience because the stakes were so much higher?

Romero: Yes, to some extent. However, for the first time, we weren't the gambler. It was all outside financing, so it wasn't our money. Still, I treated it as though it was. All that money is on the screen. We didn't take big fees or anything. We were very economical. I think that if a studio budgeted this script, they would have budgeted it at around $12 million. We had a cast of sixty under union regulations. We used a hundred bikes and twelve of the best stunt men from Stunts Unlimited to do the action sequences.

TZ: Were the stunts especially challenging to direct because of the risks involved?

Romero: For sure. I had my heart stopped a few times. But these guys were real pros. Gary Davis was the stunt coordinator, and his riders are the greatest in the world. The only injuries were minor, football-type injuries. Nobody was seriously hurt.

Knightriders is, in fact, a more delicate film than the ones I've done in the past. It has a very delicate balance between the action sequences and the characters' dramatic scenes. There's a lot of action in the film, but there's also a lot of meat, and it was difficult integrating the two. That was the real challenge.

TZ: In all of your films, you seem to have developed an ensemble of largely unknown actors. Some people have referred to it as a kind of family. Do you want to continue working with a group of this sort?

Romero: I'd love to. However, one of my next films, *Creepshow*, is going to have some names in it, because it's the kind of film that needs that sort of treatment. It's an anthology, with five separate stories—and with so much going on, you need to know a character the moment he's on the screen. In that situation, I have no objection to casting stars. What I object to is casting a name simply for the sake of the name . . . though my partner says, facetiously, that I shouldn't hold it against someone just because he has a name.

TZ: Despite the outside financing you used for *Knightriders*, you've still managed to maintain your independence of the studios, just as you have throughout your career. Is there anything that would get you to work for a major studio?

Romero: I'm the first one on the plane whenever they want to talk. I have not resisted that in any way, shape, or form. I know people at all the major studios, and I'm always in conversation with them. My problem up until now is that the only thing I've ever been offered, or the only thing I've ever shown them that they were willing to consider, have been $2-, $3-, or $4-million horror films.

The other problem with working for a studio is that I'd lose control. With a studio involved, the film is no longer mine—and yet it's my neck that's still on the line. I'm gambling that, in the long run, I'm better off working independently. My films will succeed or fail the same way, but at least they'll be my films.

TZ: What's your next film going to be?

Romero: *Creepshow*. It's written by Stephen King, and it's the first original script of his that's going to be filmed. It'll be a much bigger picture than I've done before, with a budget of between $7 and $8 million.

TZ: Aren't you also going to be doing the film of King's *The Stand*?

Romero: Yes. Steve's already written the second draft of the screenplay, but we haven't presented it to anyone. This is a project that definitely needs studio financing. It'll be a huge production, somewhere between $15 million and $20 million. However, we still want to maintain as much control as possible. We intend to package it ourselves, including the cast, and not even pitch it until we're ready to roll. Steve and I have agreed that if we can't get a deal we like, one that allows us maximum control, then we're not interested in doing it. We'll wait until we get what we want.

TZ: You two are certainly an ideal combination. How'd you get together?

Romero: I've been a fan of his forever. And I was one of the people Warner Bros. approached with *'Salem's Lot*. I immediately said yes, because I loved the property, and the conditions they were talking about seemed right. They said, "Take this book, go talk to Steve, and we don't want to see you until the movie's done. Just do it quickly." I went to Maine, and Steve and I hit it off right away. However, I never ended up making the film, because Warner Bros. got scared. They saw a lot of other vampire movies being made, and so they decided to make *Salem's Lot* for television.

TZ: I know that a great number of people, all your respective fans, are eagerly awaiting the films you'll do together.

Romero: I hope so. I know we're going to have a ball with *Creepshow*. We start shooting in July, and we plan to have it ready for release by spring of 1982.

TZ: Aside from King, are there any other horror and suspense writers whose work you admire?

Romero: I like Richard Matheson a lot, and Peter Straub, and also Ira Levin. And I enjoy the gothic writers, like Bram Stoker.

TZ: Is it true that you're writing a novel yourself?

Romero: Yes. It's about the supernatural. Right now I'm planning it just as a novel, but if I like it enough, I'll probably turn it into a movie.

TZ: As a leading practitioner of the genre, do you think the horror film will always be with us? Or will we reach a point where we become so jaded that nothing new can jolt us?

Romero: I think there are always going to be new ideas in the hopper. Who would have thought, before *Jaws*, that a shark would end up frightening everyone? When the critics speak today of the horror genre reaching a saturation point, what they're really talking about are the bad films. People are getting tired of the schlock. But there'll always be room for good, well-made films, in any genre.

TZ: One last question, and it doesn't have to do with films or books. Is there anything that scares George Romero?

Romero: Yes—the atomic bomb. Also, random violence, like what happened to John Lennon. That's what frightens me the most: real threats. I'm not scared of shadows.

The McDonaldization of America: . An Interview with George A. Romero

John Hanners and Harry Kloman/1982

From *Film Criticism* 6, no. 1 (Fall 1982): 69–81. Reprinted by permission.

George A. Romero, forty-two, made his first feature film, *Night of the Living Dead*, in 1968. Originally dismissed as a crude horror film, the work is now in the permanent collection of the Museum of Modern Art at New York. His other films included *Dawn of the Dead* (1979), *Knightriders* (1981), and *Creepshow* (1982). Born in the Bronx, he made some films as a youth with a camera given to him by a "rich uncle." Said Romero: "I never thought of filmmaking seriously, I always thought movies were made by elves at the North Pole." He studied at Pittsburgh's Carnegie-Mellon University, founding a company in Pittsburgh through which he produced and directed commercial TV spots for such clients as Calgon, Alcoa, and U.S. Steel. In the mid-1970s, he formed Laurel Entertainment with Richard Rubinstein. Romero and Rubinstein then produced many personality profiles of top sports figures for broadcast on network television. Laurel, which produced *Martin* (1977) and all of Romero's subsequent feature films, went public nearly three years ago. Romero, Rubinstein, and novelist Stephen King are currently adapting King's *The Stand* for the screen. From his Pittsburgh office, overlooking the Monongahela River, Romero discussed his independence and his work with *Film Criticism*.

FC: Let's begin by talking about your status as an independent filmmaker and your method of production. Is your way of raising money harder or easier than Hollywood's way?

GR: Hollywood's way of raising money—or an independent's way of raising money in Hollywood—in a certain sense is easier if you have a reputation. If they're inclined to give you a deal, you are really just going in and asking for a yes or no on the production of a film. But then you start buying problems immediately. If I were an independent and I wanted to go into Hollywood and say, "I just read this paperback and I really want to make this movie, will you buy the book?" they might say, "Yeah, come on out, we'll give you an office and a secretary and we'll buy the book." But they own the property and they immediately influence what they want to do with it, and their market analysts come in and they start saying, "We think that maybe we should change the ending because our guys don't feel an audience is going to like this ending." Those kinds of interferences start almost right away, which is why so many deals in Hollywood stay in development for three, four, five years—in the case of *Cuckoo's Nest*, twelve years in development. In the case of *Salem's Lot*, which Warner Bros. asked me to direct, they had already bought and paid for about eight screenplays. Everybody wrote one for that. Steve King wrote one, Stirling Silliphant, Larry Cohen, Mike Nichols, Paul Monash. There were screenplays coming out of everybody's ears and one regime moves out of the studio and a new regime moves in. And they say, "We don't like this, we think we should change the ending" or "it needs more impact in this area." A project can stay in development forever. That's a problem that has less to do with money than it does with all the lieutenants trying to justify their jobs and positions. So it all has a business base, and you can't really blame the approach of the business people who are at the top for behaving the way they do.

Getting a studio to agree to financing in a certain sense is easy because it's one-stop shopping if you walk in there with a package that's ready to shoot. Our company is public now; it has been for the last two and a half years. We're not putting money into production, but we're putting money into developing projects, so that when we walk into a studio we have a screenplay that we like already and maybe we even have a cast or parts of a cast attached to it. It's easier to raise money that way. It's easier to make a deal. What we have done in the past is put together some European money, some private money and money from theater chains. We've done most of our business with UFD, United Film Distribution, which is a subsidiary of United Artist Theaters. The Hassaneins, Salah and Richard, run that operation. We've been able to walk in and say we want to make a film, and so far they've agreed to follow our creative instincts, assuming that we could come to a business agreement with them.

In the case of *Dawn of the Dead*, which was on a $1.5 million scale, the project was really initiated by Italian director Dario Argento. He made *Bird with the Crystal Plumage* and *Deep Red*. He was a fan of *Night of the Living Dead* and knew that I was contemplating doing Part II. We showed him the script and he offered half the budget up front in exchange for the non-English language world. That's a pretty good deal, because the English language world represents more than the non-English language world. Having that money, we came back to the states and put together a group of investments—some private individuals from around here, some people from in the business, dabblers in the business—and we just literally put together the rest of the budget by going around and talking to people and raising money.

FC: Was that all Argento asked for: the non-English language world?
GR: No. He had cut on the picture above two hours. Usually this is another thing. Even when a studio says they'll give you three cuts, or six cuts, they reserve that phrase, "final cut." Those guys don't want to sit around and change your picture just for the sake of changing it. Of course, in some radical situations where, if you have agreed, you put in some particularly violent scene or some graphic sexual passage which they don't want, then they will try to influence the film itself. Mainly, they don't want to get into the kind of situation they got into with [Michael] Cimino, where you walk in with a three-and-a-half-hour film and they have no right to cut it down. Running time is what they're worried about, because the industry can't handle a long running time anymore. I disagree with that; in fact, I waved flags for more running time on films. I think that probably the biggest single problem with most of the films that are out is that they're too short.

FC: Then filmmakers don't have the time to do what they want to do?
GR: They don't have time to do anything they want to do. You can't, in ninety minutes, tell an intelligent story and be spectacular with the effects. It's been reduced down to that because of the two-hour show-time length and because of the "spill and fill" factor: they want people in and out of the theater in under two hours. They sell more candy that way, they run more shows, and they don't have to keep the theater open longer. But it's a crock, because they will keep the theater open longer for a midnight show if the film is successful. So I don't think it's meaningful. I think they're kidding themselves. Now, there are other factors. For every ten minutes of running time you have an extra reel of film. The weight of that in the shipping can is a substantial economic

factor when you start having to think about shipping 1,500 of those things around.

FC: What did it cost to distribute *Creepshow*? Couldn't you or UFD have distributed it?

GR: Sure. We could have and UFD could have. It would have cost the same amount of money to do the same kind of job. To do less—to distribute the way they did *Dawn of the Dead*—they would spend less, but they would make less. It's a question of judging how much you make because you're out there, everywhere, and because you run a network spot and because you can do a network talk show. You definitely have advantages when you are out there wide. There are also disadvantages: you won't play as long. It's a quick kill kind of philosophy.

FC: What sort of rights did you lose having a major distribute *Creepshow*?

GR: None. None. Absolutely none. But the film was finished.

FC: Is that common or is that rare?

GR: It's common for a finished picture. If you can get a picture finished, and somebody wants to distribute, you really don't have to give up anything because somebody is distributing it. Theoretically, you'll benefit by it. There were a couple of studios that came after the picture or exhibited interest, but we couldn't sell because we had nothing to do with it at that point. That was up to the Hassaneins. In fact, they were all set to distribute. They had posters up: there was a big billboard on Times Square and a big billboard on the Sunset Strip in L.A. and they all announced July 30. But at the last minute they made a deal.

FC: What other independent filmmakers do you associate with?

GR: Very few. I don't know any of them. I've met no one that's working the way I'm working. I think we're unique. The closet thing to us, I think, is probably Earl Owensby. But his operation is quick-and-dirty films targeted mostly at the Sunbelt, and it's a different ballgame. I think they're making money. I'm not decrying what they're doing. I think it's great to see that kind of stuff happening. But I don't think anyone operates quite the way we operate. I think we're the only ones that are operating with some serious capital. But we're not using that capital to produce with; we're just using it to develop projects and to keep going. Nobody in this company is getting rich on any of these pictures, because it all pumps back in. We're trying legitimately build a business and get involved in other areas. We're starting to get involved with production of films from other directors.

FC: Independents are often said to be making films Hollywood can't or won't make. Why wouldn't Hollywood make *Creepshow*?

GR: Well, in the case of *Creepshow*, we shopped at three studios and they all said no because it was an anthology. Now, today, there are six anthologies shooting. So tell me about it. It's a matter of timing. This doesn't mean this film was beyond the reach of studio comprehension in any way. They just decided they didn't want it. I mean, two studios passed up *E.T.* There is a lot of bullshit in making deals, but very often it's no different than going to get a mortgage: you might hit two banks before someone lays a mortgage on you. Of course it has a lot to do with who you know, but what that really means is that they trust you are going to deliver. And sure, some people have an inside track because you know the right people and take meetings at the Polo Lounge and all that. That makes it easier to some extent, but if you have a good reputation out there—which we do—you don't have any problems getting in doors, nor is there any automatic rejection of an idea.

FC: *Creepshow* was trimmed from your original version by ten minutes.

GR: Yes. But I wanted to trim it. I wanted to do another cut on that picture. Because of the July 30 opening date, in order to bid theaters, we had to have it finished by the end of June and we also needed it for the Cannes Festival. It was a squeaker pulling it off. January was the first time I saw the whole movie on a big screen without breaks and without looking at it on a Moviola. I wanted another month to sit with it, and I wanted to cut it, but I couldn't get the money it would have required. Then we showed it at Cannes, and we couldn't pull all that glue apart. You can't just go in with a pair of scissors and cut it here and cut it here. We had eight music tracks with really involved segues, so that if you make a cut here in the picture, now you have to slide that piece of music that way, and then this note is not hitting on the shot you want it to hit on and this piece of music slides the other way. The sound effects got really, really involved, and it's a long process to make a cut. Happily, when Warner Bros. bought it, they said almost right away they would like to wait until fall to develop their own campaign and test the picture, and basically I said, "Well, hell, if you're going to do that, will you let me make another pass at it?" And it's coincidence that it came down to under two hours. I wasn't running against my contract there, because in fact they were going to release it at 2:07.

FC: Then all the cuts were yours?

GR: The cuts were absolutely done right here in this shop, and they were all our cuts. Warner changed one thing. Adrienne [Barbeau] says at one point, at a lawn party in the picture, something about "Emily Post, Emily Vanderbilt, whoever that etiquette cunt is," and they insisted we take out the word "cunt." That was the only change Warner insisted.

FC: What do you think an independent most needs to be successful: money, a distribution network or name actors to put above the billboard?

GR: Money. No question. Name actors don't do anything in terms of box office any more today at all. They guarantee a certain amount of television revenue, that's it. It's a rare bird, like Clint Eastwood, that will still cause people to come out to the theaters. And as far as independents kicking over the system, it ain't never gonna happen. Economically, you can't make money on a small scale with a movie in this country. The small distributors have all gone belly up; there's just no competition any more. You can't get screens. It's part of the McDonaldization of America, unfortunately. A movie like *The Great Santini* made a lot of money. But it's not making a lot of money by Hollywood standards. None of these films do in Hollywood standards.

FC: But independents don't need to make as much money as Hollywood, do they?

GR: The hell you don't. We haven't gotten *Martin* into the black yet. You just can't get into the black. You can't get screens, you can't get good screens, and you can't get a good cut from the theater. You can't even get drive-ins anymore because they have *Superman III* booked in there already for 1983 and they figure it's going to play for eight months. You just can't do it.

FC: Yet you are successful.

GR: We have been successful even on the balance sheet, but we came up at a different time. It wasn't the case twelve years ago. It is the case now. Look at the kind of films that don't even get distributed: Robert

Altman's *Health* never even got distributed. The odds against making a film like *Return of the Secaucus Seven* hit are very, very slim. You know, the prints on *Creepshow* cost $2 million. It's not exactly "give me six wallet size." It's astounding. So I don't care if you make a picture for $500,000 and you try to get effective distribution from Warner Bros. You're going to pick up an automatic $8 million nut, just because they're handling it for you. Interest on $2 million, interest on the prints: forget it!

FC: Has the critical success or critical praise you've gotten for your films been a boost or a comfort to you?
GR: I'm in that weird sort of limbo, half way between good and bad. I get more bad reviews than I get good. So my tendency has been to ignore it all and not worry about it.

FC: Were there some things you might have wanted to do in *Creepshow* but couldn't because of the budget?
GR: A few things, but not much. *Creepshow* was about 95 percent what it needed to be. I would have liked a little more time for the graphics and post production.

FC: Where was the post-production done?
GR: All here [in Pittsburgh]. The animation was done here. Now the optical work—gluing it all together and matting it in—was done in New York at Computer Opticals. The matte paintings were done in L.A.

FC: When you make a film, do you have an ideal audience in mind, or do you have an audience of one?
GR: I have me. And my friends. We all sit around—Mike [cinematographer Michael Gornick], my wife, and the other editors that we work with—and bullshit about it a lot. But I guess I make my final decisions based on instinct. Not until after I'm pretty close to a final cut do I start to think about an audience, and even then it's in a broad stroke and has to do with things like, "Well, should we change this language or is this going to be too offensive?" I've never don't too much to change any of those things; we usually wound up just leaving it alone. But you can't help but have little nagging fears about that. For example, in the case of *Dawn of the Dead*, my biggest problem was not the fact that the film was likely to get an X. My biggest problem was with what an X rating would automatically do to the film's chances of success because of the punitive restrictions on a picture which has an X or which is unrated.

You can't advertise in some papers, you can't buy prime-time television advertising. In some cities, you can't buy television advertising at all. Those are really hard economic facts of life. But happily, in the case of *Dawn of the Dead*, we had the support of UFD and Sal Hassanein, and we put the picture out just the way it was, without a rating. But I object to the X rating, period; not just on my pictures, but in general.

FC: Why?

GR: Well, G is a copyrighted trademark of the MPAA. It stands for General. PG stands for Parental Guidance. R stands for Restricted. What does X stand for? It's negative. You might as well put the skull over the crossbones and say "poison." It's also not a copyrighted trademark. They never copyrighted it because they didn't want to be viewed as putting their seal of approval on somebody's motel movies. And so anybody can use the X. You can use X, double X, triple X, and people that want it just use it. As far as I'm concerned, no legitimate distributor or producer will use the X anymore, because it doesn't exist. It doesn't have the same dignity as the other ratings. As a result, R is the stiffest rating that we have which has dignity and which is legitimate. So if somebody comes in who is serious-minded and makes a film that has enough clout, they can appeal and get more explicit material squeezed into a R. As a result, more explicit material gets squeezed into PG. Audiences don't get pissed off because X-rated movies exist: they get pissed off when they put kids in the station wagon and go see a PG picture and are exposed to nudity and language. I think they need an Adults Only rating that has the same dignity as the other ratings and then expand everything back out that way. And of course G is in limbo. Nobody wants a G. They wrote the arm-slash scene into *Star Wars*, so the story goes, so that they'd get a PG.

FC: At times you called your films "roller coaster rides," while at other timers you've called them "moral plays" with horror as a vehicle for your message. Can you resolve that?

GR: What the surface of a movie does for most people is provide a roller coaster ride, and I've actually seen that accurately quoted in a couple of places. But I believe—and I've been attacked for this—I believe that most of the audience really doesn't care about what might lie underneath or what moral might be there. I believe most audiences today go to the movies almost like going to Mass. It's more ritualistic, and in an extreme case, like *Rocky Horror Picture Show*, it becomes all ritual. To that extent, holding the roller coaster ride on the surface of the film is most important to people that go to see it. Maybe something about the underbelly sticks. Maybe something about the moral sticks. You know, maybe. And that's why I never wanted to go make a movie about some crazed killer that went off and slashed up fourteen girls in a girls' camp. I think people who defend those movies for what they might have underneath are defending something which almost all horror has. That only point I see about those films at all is that maybe, maybe there's a kind of morality line which runs through them which has to do with the viewers that go see them admiring the fact the characters are being punished for liberal sexual behavior. And maybe there's a little bit of an outcry which is saying, "Hey, spank me." Maybe. I tend to doubt it.

FC: Some of the "slasher" or "terror" films have been called dangerous, even anti-feminist. I wonder if you share that view, and if you think they give films like yours a bad frame of reference? Will people fail to see the difference between *Creepshow* and *Don't Answer the Phone* or *Friday the 13th*?

GR: I think that a taint has been put on the genre by those films. And I think, by and large, people tend to lump horror films into a single category. And that bothers me a little. There have been a lot of bad films made by people that really don't care about the genre or don't have any love or respect for it. I swear, you could set up a business just producing slasher scenes and selling them off like stock footage.

FC: You seem to have an anti-institutional bias, both in terms of the themes of your films and your method of production. *Dawn of the Dead* sends up commercialism, *Knightriders* is all about outsiders, and the last segment of *Creepshow* is brilliant in that regard.

GR: That's Steve's (screenwriter Stephen King), you know. I would have shot Steve's script no matter what he wrote because that was the deal we had. I respect Steve's work a lot, and this was really a celebration of the EC Comic stories. I wasn't in this for any kind of emotional underbelly. This was a pure job of execution. It was getting a chance to work with somebody else's viewpoint. But I guess I have a little bit of irreverence that comes through in my work. It's the way I think, I guess. It just comes out.

FC: Could you comment on your method of filming. Your camera moved about seven or eight times in two hours of *Creepshow*. Otherwise, it was all framing.

GR: What I really wanted to do was to make it completely static, like a comic book. We didn't want to do a lot of camera tricks. But my tendency is not to move the camera. I don't ask Mike (Gornick) to do a lot of moving the camera. I'm not enraptured by fancy shots. I will never in my life—I shouldn't say this—well, maybe once in my life I'll do a shot like the opening shot in *Touch of Evil*. But I'm not enraptured by it as an essential part of the form.

FC: What does excite you cinematically?

GR: This is going to sound obscure, but it excites me most when I don't recognize the technique. If a film really cooks, the first few times I see it I won't be able to tell you what happens. It's always that emotion, that ritual. The shower sequence in *Psycho* is all largely static shots. Editing, that was done with editing. I just can't see myself licking off four days of rehearsal when you're running fifty grand a day to make one shot. Then you get it back to the editing table and you don't have any options. I like to shoot really fast, and I like to have as much material as possible. I don't shoot master shots. I shoot the equivalent of a master shot in the opening of a scene to establish place, but I don't—I'm afraid of them, man. Because I know some completion bonder or somebody is going to show up and say, "Well, we're out of time, Jack. That's your scene." I'd rather be able to say I don't have it all yet, and literally not have it. When you have it in a master, you can't quite say you don't have it.

I don't know what sense it makes if you dolly up this way and curve around this way and see people moving out. What does it do for anything, unless somebody really uses that as an aesthetic? John Carpenter uses that better than anyone I've seen. The scenes in *Halloween* are brilliant. John knows how to use that, and it's all very calculated. In a lot of films, the shots are being done just to do it. It's just somebody flexing his craft approach. It becomes the start of the art and then it gets overused and then you get fucking tired of it. If I see one more Steady-Cam . . .

FC: How important is it for the government to get involved in the arts? Is there more of a need in America for something like the Film Board of Canada?

GR: That's a tough one. I wish there was some subsidy that didn't come through Hollywood. The American Film Institute is well and good, but AFI is really a propaganda mechanism for the mainstream in a certain sense. I should clarify that: I think what AFI does is very positive, but it has a single-minded kind of dedication. So would government subsidy to a certain extent. In Canada, it creates an industry that can provide work for a lot of people. It can give people the ability to use the hardware, to get out and develop as technicians, because you really have to learn to use the pencil before you can start to draw. But there has not been a Canadian film that has gone out and made any money. So what happens, I think, is that there's a great deal of masturbation out there. It's not facing the real problem of the business and therefore is not really effecting change in a meaningful way. I guess I'm a believer in effecting change from the inside.

FC: You don't see any hope of developing an audience for the small picture, like *Secaucus Seven* or *Heartland*?
GR: I really don't. I don't have enough faith in the audience. Number one, I don't think they're experimenting any more or are willing to try anything new. They respond to peer pressure, they respond to advertising, they respond to whatever's hot, whatever cuts though the white noise—just as they do with literature, blue jeans, hamburgers, and everything else. Even genres that should be popular, like thrillers, nobody wants to see any more.

FC: Will horror stick around as a genre?
GR: I think it will. It's been around forever, even before Hollywood started to make it an "A" feature. Horror and fantasy are real close. They're kind of horns on the same goat. And there's the supernatural and gothic stuff, and science fiction.

FC: Do you see yourself as a gothic filmmaker?
GR: I see myself as having gothic roots, anyway.

FC: Can you cite some influences?
GR: Influences stylistically, yes. Content, no. stylistically, as far as film form, I love Val Lewton's *Cat People* (1942). I guess I really like Orson Welles's films a lot. And I love Howard Hawks and Michael Powell. I probably watched Powell's *Tales of Hoffman* (1953) when I was a kid more than anything. It's a ballet, an opera, but it's fantasy all the way and it's gorgeous. That film probably had the strongest influence on me of any film I've ever seen.

FC: What's in your future? We know you're working on *The Stand*.

GR: Yes, *The Stand* is huge. I think the problem is that people in Hollywood put it on their postal scale instead of opening the cover.

FC: Do you worry about being misunderstood by the audience? Again, someone coming out of *Dawn of the Dead* and saying, "Gee, that's the best movie I've seen since *Friday the 13th*?"
GR: That bothers me, sure. But I don't worry about it. I expect it. If the film is out there and it's talking to people and there are some people noticing what's underneath it, that's cool. In a certain sense, it's part personal gratification. None of us working in this medium is lacking in terms of ego gratification. Anybody that says they are is crazy. It's the most ego-gratifying medium that you can be in. You really have to turn it off. You start believing you own shit. [laughs] Wishes and intents. For example, I like Paul Mazursky's work. But as far as I'm concerned, he doesn't have to be making a film. He can do what he does in print. And that doesn't excite me at all. *An Unmarried Woman* doesn't need to be a movie in order for its message to get out. The fact that you're filming isn't really cinema craft. In fact, the craftsmanship level in that film is pretty low.

FC: Can you name some contemporary directors you like craftwise as well as storywise?
GR: Zinnemann. Schlesinger. Ken Russell. Craftwise, I think Spielberg is a genius. I think Spielberg really knows how to glue that shit together. Kubrick used to be my main man. I love most of his work. I haven't liked all his recent stuff.

FC: In film, can style be the substance?
GR: I don't think it is the substance. You're talking about two different things. You're talking about somebody who writes his own material and controls the whole thing from the jump. And it's really two different jobs. Very often it synchronizes. I respect Spielberg's *1941* on a craft level, but it's a bag of shit. I don't think style is substance at all—except maybe in *Fantasia*, something which is designed to grow out of what the style is. If you're going to be a craftsman or a hired gun, then your job is to translate the ideas of the author rather than superimposing your own ideas. I see pitifully little discussion of that situation. And there's this immediate sort of rush to judgment whenever a film comes out about how Schlesinger would have us believe blah blah blah. Selling is the job of the director. It's like making a commercial. You know,

"I'm going to make this cake of soap look like heaven." Timing, pacing, standing the dialogue and just not letting it sit there. That's craft, but that doesn't change the overall message.

FC: Are these sorts of decisions conscious or instinctual on the part of the director?

GR: Oh, I don't know. On the set, and most sets I've been on, you don't sit around and overanalyze. Sometimes actors are serious about it, so you wind up having discussions about craft and performance and vocal style and pace. But it's pretty much instinctive. Because no matter how much film I shoot, I never know what it's going to look like until I glue it together. Working with Hal Holbrook [in *Creepshow*] was an extraordinary revelation. Because there were scenes we shot where I would be as close to him as I am to you right now and even at that distance I couldn't see everything he was doing. Only when he was up there ten feet high could I see what was going on in his face—little eye movements and things I wouldn't even catch on the set. And I like to be able to use that.

FC: Susan Sontag said that science fiction, and perhaps other generic forms, while they raise serious concerns, are "inadequate responses" to the concerns they raise because they tend to be formulaic or are subject to formulaic criticisms. How do you respond to that?

GR: Maybe that's true, but I think it's only true for a very small portion of the audience. I don't think they will reach that far, nor do I think that it's inadequately educating them. We have to speak in terms that are recognizable and understandable. And I don't think that it has to be realistic or contemporary in order to do that. In fact, I think you have the reverse. If you make a film like *Saturday Night Fever*, no matter what your intention, you're going to have twenty million people the next week who are dressing that way and dancing that way. To me, that's real behavior manipulation. And I think in that sense it might be just as valid.

George Romero on Directing
Day of the Dead

Paul Gagne/1985

From *Cinefantastique* 15, no. 6 (1985): 49. Reprinted by permission.

Shortly before the release of *Day of the Dead*, director George Romero resigned from active participation in Laurel Productions. Partnered with producer Richard Rubinstein, Laurel produced *Day of the Dead* as well as earlier Romero films *Martin*, *Dawn of the Dead*, and *Creepshow*. Romero remains a stockholder in the company and is still contractually committed to Laurel to direct Stephen King's *Pet Sematary* as well as a project developed with Marvel Comics.

Now a free agent, Romero is seeking representation in Hollywood and assignments on non-Laurel productions. The longtime Pittsburgh resident has also recently relocated to Florida, on the island where they filmed *Day of the Dead*.

The following interview by Paul Gagne is excerpted from a forthcoming issue to be devoted to "The Films of George Romero."

Paul Gagne: At what point did the zombie "trilogy" become a trilogy?

George Romero: Right away. It always was, in my mind. There were always three parts to the story. They weren't dominant. All three parts were at the farmhouse. The third part was just a paragraph or two

It was a story I wrote before I ever started to write the *Night of the Living Dead* screenplay; a couple of years before that. I started to take the first part of it and turn it into a screenplay. There wasn't really very much detail in it. Jack Russo took over at some point after we started to shoot. But I never anticipated doing three movies, let alone four, or whatever else this may become!

Gagne: Is *Day of the Dead* starting to spark any interest in a fourth picture?

Romero: No, I don't think so. I have kind of a sick feeling that it might not. It's not gonna get a huge release.

United Film Distributors is only going to work a few hundred prints. They can never be competitive with advertising, partly because it's unrated and partly because UFD is such a small company—they can't compete with Paramount; the big boys. So I don't know how long the film can survive against big product. None of them have ever had a wide audience. They have a kind of loyal cadre of people that keep coming back to support them. On that small scale Salah Hassanein at UFD has been able to make some money on them, but they don't go out and blow the roof off.

Also, I don't know whether it will pull an audience.

Gagne: The three zombie films are very different in texture. *Night of the Living Dead* has a gritty harsh realistic quality; *Dawn of the Dead* is flashier, more comic book and slapstick. How do you compare *Day of the Dead* with the others?

Romero: I think it is a lot closer to *Dawn of the Dead* simply because Mike Gornick shot it, so it has a lot of his style layered on top of it. Its tone isn't quite as bawdy. It's not as silly. It's really harsh. It's very arch—the characters are bigger and broader than life, but it's still pretty light-hearted and good-natured! I think it's very accessible. It's kind of eighties idiomatic, almost like a video, in a way. Very fast-paced.

Gage: So the eighties have crept in.

Romero: With the original script that was more inherent in the material. I'm just talking about texture. I always liked the idea that the first film reflected the late sixties in personality, and the second one the mid-seventies. And this one might have an eighties personality; it sort of does, texturally.

Gagne: Producer Richard Rubinstein maintains that in cutting down the original *Day of the Dead* script, you eliminated a lot of material that would only have wound up on the cutting room floor, anyway.

Romero: That's misleading; the script is not a cut-down. It's a completely different script. I backed up in time. I went back to a point where this military team was first sent down into this cave. I wrote out a character named Balthesar and a sort of civilian contingent. I took it back to a point where the scientists first got the bright idea to feed the zombies. It's a completely different script, and this script was never longer than eighty-eight pages. It's *not* a cut-down script. I changed it, and it was really a wrenching, radical change in my mind. And I only had about three weeks to do it.

Gagne: If you shot the original script, would it have been three hours?

Romero: It would have been long; there's no question about that. But I did an on-paper edit of that script at 204 pages and ultimately got it down to 122 pages—something like that. With a fine edit that's a two-hour film.

Gagne: You've mentioned that you regard a zombie, Bub, as the film's central character.

Romero: Yeah, even though Sarah's character (acted by Lori Cardille) represents the audience. Everything happens through her eyes. But in terms of the films collectively, I think Bub's the key. He ain't nothin' more than a misunderstood monster! Howard Sherman just did such a wonderful job with the part.

Gage: I understand Howard Sherman had an interesting audition.

Romero: He brought props—a turkey leg!—and he was just great. He's a wonderful mime, and that's what you have to be to do the zombies really well. Some of the stuff he does is so subtle that you can watch it and watch it and it keeps getting better.

Gagne: Is Lori Cardille the daughter of "Chilly Billy" Cardille, the Pittsburgh television host of *Chiller Theatre* who appeared in *Night of the Living Dead*?

Romero: Yeah! I've know her dad for a long time. It's delightful to me that he's in *Night of the Living Dead*. I'm delighted to have Lori in this film. Bill was a real supporter of ours in those days, and he really kept us going. He would talk about us on the air a lot, and I think he had a lot to do with our ability to ultimately raise money and finish the movie. Simply because he would talk about us to his audience. It gave us that extra bit of credibility. Plus he came out and was in the film— and brought the news guys from the station and some valuable props that we couldn't afford!

George Romero: Monkeying with Horror

Frederick C. Szebin/1988

From *Cinefantastique* 18, no. 4 (1988): 21, 55.

No one is openly willing to call George Romero's latest film *Monkey Shines* a horror movie. "It's more of a thriller," said star Jason Beghe. "It's about a love bond that becomes very distorted."

Romero, known for his ghastly images of blasted bodies and disembowlings, doesn't refer to it as a horror film either. "I'm hoping the last half hour will be pretty intense," he said. "But it's not bloody." Though the makeup master of grue, Tom Savini, is working on the film, Romero said there's hardly enough to keep Savini busy.

Monkey Shines, a $6 million production which Orion plans to release this summer, is Romero's first film in two years, since *Day of the Dead* completed the Pittsburgh-based filmmaker's highly touted and controversial zombie trilogy. *Monkey Shines* is based on a novel by Michael Stewart and stars Beghe as a quadriplegic with an experimental, specially trained, genetically altered Capuchin monkey helpmate. After Beghe develops a psychic bond with the animal, those who frustrate or hurt the invalid begin to turn up dead under mysterious circumstances. The idea of placing a Capuchin monkey, the pet of old-time street-corner organ grinders, with a quadriplegic may seem outrageous at first, but the Boston-based project, Helping Hands, has been doing just that for several years.

Romero's name has been associated with a number of genre projects since he severed his working relationship with Laurel Entertainment after *Day of the Dead*. (Romero retains co-ownership with former partner Richard Rubinstein). Romero's new-found free agent status brought several projects his way, including *Turn of the Screw* for Columbia, an adaptation of Richard Bachman's *The Long Walk*, and remakes of perennial classics *The Mummy* and *War of the Worlds* (for Universal and Paramount respectively). Most of the projects remain in development, but Romero's *War of the Worlds* feature, which he was set to direct, seems still-born with the announcement by Paramount of plans for a syndicated TV series in the mold of *Star Trek—The Next Generation*, geared for a fall 1988 air date.

In the midst of his busy writing schedule, *Monkey Shines* offered Romero an almost immediate production opportunity for his Florida-based Sanebel Films company. The film's fourteen-week shooting schedule was spent in Pittsburgh and at Romero's Coraopolis studio, with additional exteriors lensed in Carnegie. Like most of Romero's previous work, the film features a talented, but primarily unknown cast, including Jason (*1ˢᵗ and 10*) Beghe, John (*To Live and Die in L.A.*) Pankow, Kate (*North and South: Book II*) McNeil, and veteran actress Joyce Van Patten. Also, Romero's wife Chris follows her appearances in *Dawn of the Dead*, *Knightriders*, and *Creepshow* with a featured role as Beghe's nurse.

With *Monkey Shines* awaiting release, it may seem like an opportune time for Romero to commence the oft-announced but never instigated lensing of two of Stephen King's still-unfilmed works, *Pet Sematary* and *The Stand*. Despite completed scripts and a yearning on Romero's part, neither novel has received the cinematic treatment for a very simple reason. "Both projects are still at Laurel and I have first refusal to direct both of them," he said. "There's been a completed script for *The Stand* for over two years which Steve [King] and I worked on a little together, but it's his script all the way. Unfortunately, there was a rash of Stephen King films that did not sell a lot of tickets at the box office.

"*The Stand* was always huge and very expensive, at least $20 million," Romero continued. "Had a couple of movies based on Steve's books gone through the roof, I think we could have financed it in a minute. It's no fault of the material, even though I didn't think all the films were very good. It's just circumstance. And I'm dying to film *Pet Sematary*, but Laurel hasn't been able to get a deal structured. I even did storyboards and was ready to go. There was a deal set up, but it just fell apart at the last minute."

One film that Romero has never planned to make is the persistently rumored fourth chapter in his zombie series, *Twilight of the Dead*. This pseudo-project was supposed to allow him to make the film that *Day of the Dead* was to be before drastic budget cuts necessitated rewrites that changed its perspective. "*Twilight of the Dead* was never real," Romero insisted. "It was a project that was suggested to me by other people. I may have joked about it, but I never had any intention of doing it." However, Romero is considering producing a remake of the original *Night of the Living Dead*, with Tom Savini as director.

Romero's next project looks to be *Apartment Living*, a horror-comedy created by Warren Hite, with a script by Hite and Romero, polished by Joe Stillman for Saratoga Films. The story concerns a beautifully kept apartment building in a decaying neighborhood that houses mostly retirees which turns out to be a living entity that maintains itself and sustains the elderly within, some of whom are well over a hundred years old. To maintain this capability, the building needs a periodic feeding and will go to great lengths to perpetuate itself. Pre-production is scheduled for May with a June start date on Florida and Pittsburgh locations for release by New Century/Vista.

George Romero vs. Hollywood

Dennis Fischer/1989

From *Cinefantastique* 19, no. 3 (1989): 36–37. Reprinted by permission.

Though critics found favor with *Monkey Shines*, the latest themati-
cally ambitious horror effort from director George Romero, audiences shunned the film when Orion Pictures opened it last summer. For
Romero, the maverick independent filmmaker who made a name for
himself directing *Night of the Living Dead* and other low-budget shock-
ers in Pittsburgh, the film was a move up to the majors, working for
producer Charles Evans, the man who backed *Tootsie*. Nevertheless,
Romero chose to shoot the film on Pittsburgh's home ground.

Working for Hollywood, Romero didn't enjoy the kind of control
and creative independence he was used to. Prior to release, Evans and
Orion insisted on the filming of a new ending, a tacky, *Carrie*-inspired
dream sequence jolt, much to Romero's dismay. "If it was just me and
my movie," said Romero, "I would not have changed it."

Romero's original ending involved Burbage, the university research
supervisor played by Stephen Root, one of the character threads in
Romero's script, based on the book by Michael Stewart. Burbage is head
of the science department where researcher John Pankow develops the
serum that turns paraplegic friend Jason Beghe's capuchin monkey
helpmate into a super-intelligent, psychically-bonded killer. In the film,
Romero established Burbage as an unpleasant character whose cruel approach to the scientific method results in unnecessary torturing of lab
animals, raising the ire of anti-vivisectionists. The animal rights activ-
ists make a brief appearance at the beginning, spray-painting slogans
on Pankow's door. Romero provides clear indications that Burbage has
been meddling with Pankow's experiment and Romero sets the scene
for his comeuppance, but it never arrives in the film in its current form
because of the changes that were made.

"I had an ending on the picture which just continued the experiment," said Romero. "It was a little coda which was less than a minute long. It conveyed that Dean Burbage has got the experimental serum and the other monkeys and plans to continue the experiment."

Romero said his lost ending picked up after a shot of Beghe driving away happily with girlfriend Melanie Parker. "You see Burbage driving to the university and the three protesters have now turned into a couple of hundred," Romero said, describing the scene. "They're a lot more violent. They throw things at him. He gets hit with a rock and turns around and he's got this maniacal look on his face and says, 'You deserve whatever you get.' He goes back to the refrigerator in the lab and you see he has several dozen vials of serum. You see this sort of *Re-Animator* type effect of him loading the syringe and suddenly a monkey jumps on his shoulder and he's bleeding from a cut. He turns to the camera and the monkey licks the blood off his forehead. I did a really campy fade-out on it. It was tongue-in-cheek, sort of a signature. It was something I liked a lot. We did light cues on the set, almost *Creepshow*-type light cues."

The finished film was previewed for audiences with Romero's ending, and that's when the trouble began.

"As a result of the preview screenings, which is the way of doing things out here [in Hollywood], we got hundreds of people responding negatively to that ending," said Romero. "It wasn't violently negative, it was just that when asked 'What did you like least about the picture?' uniformly that last scene came up for various reasons. People felt that Burbage wasn't an important enough character to bring back, they didn't like the light cues, etc.

"This whole preview process I think is flawed," continued Romero. "When you ask someone, 'What's the scene you liked least?' you could show them *Casablanca* and they'll come up with half a dozen different scenes they liked least. What are you supposed to do? Take them out even if they make literal sense? I don't agree with the basic process, but unless you're lucky enough to have that magic final cut, there's not really much you can do."

Romero said the studio didn't pressure him to change his ending. "Orion was great about this," said Romero. "They didn't put the thumbscrews on and say, 'Change this!' It just became sort of an overwhelming corporate fiscal responsibility to do something about it. The producers and the people from Orion and all sort of corporate overseers suddenly turn around and look at you and say, 'Well, you've got to do something about this.' It's pretty hard to resist the suggestion that you should change it, because they're getting this 70 percent response to it."

To punch up the ending, Romero added a shock dream sequence of a monkey bursting through Beghe's back during the operation to cure his paralysis. Commented Romero, "I don't particularly like that, but I can understand that it really works. That was something else that tested so overwhelmingly positive that it was like, 'What are you going to do?'"

Despite the contretemps, Romero said he was happy with the film overall. "I'd say, by and large, the film has pretty much the stamp of my personality on it, certainly as much as any of the things I did at Laurel," said Romero. "I was able to do it as close as possible to my concept." Romero said he had no problems collaborating closely on the script with Evans and executive producers Peter Grunwald and Gerald S. Paonessa. It was Paonessa who brought the project to Romero. "We worked very closely on the script," said Romero. "It made it a slightly slower process, but we didn't have any big, cataclysmic creative differences, so that was pretty comfortable."

One regrettable result of his *Monkey Shines* experience, however, was the loss of an opportunity for Romero to direct Stephen King's *Pet Sematary* for Laurel Productions and Paramount release. Though Romero is no longer active in running Laurel's operation, he still owns an interest in the company and has contractual obligations to fulfill on some projects. When Laurel's financing on *Pet Sematary* fell into place, Romero was busy making the changes necessary on *Monkey Shines*. Though Romero had spent a year preparing Stephen King's script for shooting, director Mary Lambert had to be brought in as his replacement when the start of production couldn't be postponed.

Romero is still hoping to make a film based on Stephen King's *The Stand* for Laurel. "Steve wrote the original screenplay and Richard [Rubinstein, Romero's Laurel partner] has commissioned another one," said Romero.

Also cancelled was the start of production on *George Romero's Apartment Living*, a project Romero was to film following *Monkey Shines*. The Saratoga Films production, written by Warren Hite and Romero, was to have been distributed by New Century/Vista, a company whose poor box office performance resulted in a cash flow shortage last year that reportedly caused the cancellation of its planned release schedule (notably, the in-the-can *Fright Night 2*).

Romero said that he is increasingly thwarted by the fact that many of the ideas he has for films he knows he won't be able to sell. Hollywood studios, according to Romero, are interested only in "high con-cept" films, a term he said means that the plot can be summed up in *TV Guide* in one sentence.

"It's the most frustrating thing about trying to get money out of this town," said Romero. "The problem with the people at the studios is either they want something that is the same as *Rambo*, or they want something that is *completely* different, but nothing in the middle. They won't or are unable to distinguish between this, that, and the other thing. The only way to raise money is privately, out in the middle of the country, where you don't have to go through that process, which is the way we used to do things."

In an effort to find different ways of producing films, Romero has started an outfit called Tartan Films association with the Theatre De-partment of Pittsburgh's Carnegie-Mellon University. Tartan will pro-duce films for distribution using "the alumni, the man-power of the school, including the arms and legs of the students and faculty, and its physical plant, to cut costs and do some things that would be nor-mally difficult to mount," said Romero. "We'll make movies or televi-sion shows or films for cassette and distribute them for profit with the idea that the profits will be pumped back into the film and television program at the school."

Romero's partners in the venture include his wife, actress Christine Forrest, who played the acerbic nurse in *Monkey Shines*, and another husband-and-wife team, Cletus and Barbara Anderson, who have often worked for Romero as production designer and costumer, respectively. "We feel that by using the school, we can cut 40 to 60 percent of the costs, so we could produce very efficiently and inexpensively. Hope-fully, whatever we do goes out and makes a couple dollars to help the school. That's what it's about."

George A. Romero

Stanley Wiater/1992

From *Dark Visions: Conversations with the Masters of the Horror Film* (New York: Avon, 1992), 147–57. Reprinted by permission.

Although George A. Romero is undoubtedly one of the most effective horror directors working today, he also happens to be one of the nicest to meet with in person. In spite of a number of successful movies in the genre, he will probably forever be known for his first feature, the 1968 classic, *Night of the Living Dead.* Independently made on a shoestring and produced in his hometown of Pittsburgh, the film has gone on to influence an entire generation of horror filmmakers.

Just as important, the fifty-year-old Romero is also known as a fiercely independent filmmaker—in more ways than one. Although he has been tempted to "go Hollywood," he has in fact made only two films that were directly distributed by major studios: *Creepshow* and *Monkey Shines.* For the most part he has worked outside of the Hollywood "system," preferring to make his own movies in his own way, most often still in Pittsburgh.

Even if he is best known for his *Dead* trilogy (which includes *Dawn of the Dead* and *Day of the Dead*), Romero has directed several other influential films, such as his modern-day interpretation of vampirism, *Martin,* and the little-seen *The Crazies.* As a screenwriter, Romero has also been involved with several popular movies, including *Creepshow 2* and *Tales from the Darkside: The Movie.* He always seems to be working.

In spite of his continuing success as a consummate filmmaker (he also has worked as cinematographer and editor on several of his films), Romero takes his enviable position in the field with an easygoing grace. Like his friend and colleague Stephen King, Romero is very much aware of his good fortune and, if anything, is too modest about his considerable accomplishments. A fine book on his career is Paul R. Gagne's *The Zombies That Ate Pittsburgh: The Films of George A. Romero.*

I spoke with Romero while he was working as executive producer (with friend Tom Savini directing) on the color remake to *Night of the Living Dead*.

Wiater: Considering the original film is now regarded as a bona fide classic, why remake *Night of the Living Dead* now?

Romero: I never wanted to do it; I just sort of went along with the people who own the property. John Russo and I own the literary rights, and there's a group of shareholders who comprise Image Ten; the company that produced the original picture. Most of these people are still alive, and they've been ripped off a million different ways on the original film. And they decided they wanted to do a remake before someone else did it. So basically I just went along with it—the way I went along with the colorized version. Then I decided to be more involved rather than not, and wrote the screenplay.

But it certainly is not something that I wanted to do, or wanted to direct; it's something that I've done already. That's pretty much it. Hopefully everybody can make a buck on it.

Wiater: At the same time you're working as executive producer on *Night of the Living Dead*, you're completing the screenplay for your next assignment, as writer and director of Stephen King's *The Dark Half*. How much time did you have to script the adaptation?

Romero: Well, I actually wrote it in finished form—that is, in the word processor in script format—in about three weeks. I kept notebooks on it. The standard screenplay commission is three months; you can get more or you can get less. Nobody breaks your knees! [Laughs.] So it's usually whatever it takes to do it right, especially if it's a fairly important project. I find that when adapting something, three months is enough. It's a lot more difficult to write something from scratch; it takes a lot longer. With an adaptation, it's pretty easy: somehow all those little switches inside your head that say, Well, it's not me, I won't blame me for this change, click in, and you breeze through it a little easier.

Wiater: We first met over a decade ago, and at that time, I had to ask the question, "When are you going to make Stephen King's *The Stand*?" Forgive me if I repeat that question, but people, are still hoping to see that happen. Will it?

Romero: Beats me. The problem is, I don't own it anymore. My ex-partner, Richard Rubenstein, owns all the properties that we had owned together. He owns them as Laurel Entertainment. Theoretically, I was scheduled to do *The Stand*. I was also scheduled to do *Pet Sematary*, but that didn't work out because there was a scheduling conflict with *Monkey Shines*. I still would have liked to have done *Pet Sematary*, but it wasn't meant to be. And as far as *The Stand*, I don't know. I know that Richard has been having screenplays done, but I haven't seen any of them. The screenplay that I saw last was one that Steve had done, and I did a little bit of cut and paste on it. I didn't write anything, but I did a little editing work just to give Steve my thoughts on what we could take out and how we could move things around a little bit. I forget what we came out with, but it was long. I think we came out with around 150 pages, maybe 160 pages. At that time of course that was what was preventing it from being made. No one wants to make a long movie that's going to cost $40 million.

Wiater: Yet that's not really a ridiculous amount, considering the epic scope of the novel.

Romero: Steve and I always maintained that it wouldn't necessarily cost $40 million; that if we could do it efficiently with a generous schedule, and with a cast that wasn't costing us $800,000 a week, that we could probably do it for a lot less. But unfortunately what happens with movies is that there's going to be a certain amount of money invested. And the producers feel they have to protect that investment by investing even more in things like stars . . . and so you know it just mushrooms. Maybe somehow Richard will be able to get it made. If he gets a deal on it, maybe he'll even talk to me about doing it, but he's not obligated to, legally. So I don't know. It could well go off without my being attached to it at all, and probably will.

Wiater: Then I'm curious to know how you became involved with *Tales from the Darkside: The Movie*, which was a Laurel production. For that film you adapted King's short story "The Cat from Hell."

Romero: I had nothing to do with that film whatsoever. Right after the original *Creepshow*, Steve agreed to do *Creepshow II*. Not to do the screenplay, but he contributed five stories. A couple of them were published stories, "The Cat from Hell" and "The Raft," and a couple of them were just idea sketches that he had. From that material I wrote a screenplay for *Creepshow II*, which was composed of five stories and a wraparound, just like the original *Creepshow*. And of course I was working for the company, Laurel, so they owned it. I imagine they had the same deal with Steve where they just owned the material. So when Richard finally made *Creepshow II*, he only used three of the stories, so now he has two stories, just sitting in the drawer, that he owns. So he put one in *Tales from the Darkside: The Movie*, and as I understand it, he has the other one in a screenplay for *Creepshow III*. So he gets his mileage from this stuff.

Wiater: You've written the screenplays for practically all your motion pictures. Have you developed a standard method for writing scripts over the past twenty years that always just works for you?

Romero: I find that what happens to me—particularly as I get older— is that I just don't have the energy to devote the whole block of time, the whole three or four months scheduled, completely to it. I often thought about writing a novel, but then I realize what a commitment that is. Screenplays are in fact about one-third the size. On the other hand, they do need more careful outlining, because they are much more concise. They're not as forgiving in terms of letting you roam. So I find that it's a process that's sort of like doing a jigsaw puzzle. It requires a certain period of really concentrated thought, which has more to do with organizing and trying to figure out what's really important. Every writer goes through that. Then the actual physical writing—particularly dialogue—what I do is usually leave all the dialogue until the end and try not to think about it; to try not to constipate the dialogue. I find that if I get preconceived speeches in my head, then I start refining them and pretty soon they sound like people. So I let that go as sort of that final coat, which is that three- or four-week period when I actually put it into the proper format in the word processor. That's working from notes and whatever else, little thoughts and ideas. I have a portable tape recorder in my car. And I'll just jot things. This has probably evolved through convenience, because I just want more time with my family. I find that when I am in the final stage of writing I very often actually have to move out of the house. We have two houses, so I'm lucky that way. But if we're all in Florida, I'll just go and rent a joint on the beach and sit there and eat Spam until I'm finished.

Wiater: Do you keep making horror movies because you truly love the genre? Or do you keep making horror movies because it's a pretty safe bet it will keep you in Spam?

Romero: Well, it's a little deeper than that. I mean, I don't think anyone will hire me for other genres. My wife and I bought the rights to a novel, which is nonhorror, and I wrote the screenplay, which I really like a lot. I've gotten a lot of phone calls from people: saying, "Gee, that's a wonderful screenplay," but that's about as far as it goes.

Now, there are a few groups that have faith in me and will give me a shot at other things. I'm hoping that one of these days we will make one of those projects into a film, rather than just a commissioned screenplay. But the answer to that is that people are not generally going to call me up unless it's horror related. Although, since *Monkey Shines*, they will now call me up with suspense stories or with real-life, non-supernatural, nonhorror thrillers. Aside from that, I do love it. I really *do* love it! [Laughs.] It's been my ticket to ride. And with horror, you can tell parables, and that's a lot harder to do with a straight thriller.

It's much harder to take a parable and squeeze it into a real-life story. Whereas with supernatural material you can make anything happen so as to fit in the notion that you want to fit between the lines. You can go back and forth between the text and subtext much more freely! It's a bonus in this genre, which I rather freely have done over the years.

Wiater: Wes Craven has also stated that he finds it all but impossible to get a project underway unless it's more or less directly horror-related. He also would like to stretch his talents, but he's stereotyped by the industry.
Romero: It's pretty frustrating. I do find myself pretty angry and much less civil than I used to be when faced with those situations. It's just not worth it anymore.

Wiater: But overall, are you satisfied with your work? You've pretty much thumbed your nose at the Hollywood establishment and, like Frank Sinatra, been able to say "I did it my way," haven't you?
Romero: Every week you get some new understanding about how some part of this business works. I'm sort of happy with my view of things, of the business side of it. I'm very unhappy with some of my work. I don't think that I have yet made a film where I've had the money or time to execute it exactly the way I would want to execute it. I'd like to do that sometime.

Wiater: Any film that still stands out as perhaps coming closest to your initial vision?
Romero: Strangely, a little film I made called *Martin*, which was a $275,000 production, comes closest in terms of the finished product to

what my conception was going in. That's because all of us were working on that out of dedication. It was one of those little films that we went out with nine people and made a movie. It didn't matter if we had to shoot at night, we shot at night. We were just there to get the movie done. I had the most freedom on that film that I've had on any of the other ones.

Wiater: Yet you've had some fairly decent budgets on a few of your projects, haven't you?

Romero: *Creepshow* was the most expensive film that I've made to date. Actually, I guess *Monkey Shines* was a little more expensive. But in both of those, there were external factors that kept me from being able to do exactly what I wanted to do. In the case of *Creepshow*, we could have used a lot more money, and even though it had a very long production schedule, it needed more time to do optical effects. It wasn't quite there; we came close, but it wasn't one hundred percent. In *Monkey Shines*, it was mostly the monkeys, and again the time to execute it properly. *Monkey Shines* is pretty successful in terms of what it was supposed to be. But we lost so much time and energy to the monkeys, and to other external factors such as disagreements amongst the producers; none of it was bad intentioned, but it got in the way.

And when you lose time, you lose time and never get it back again.

Wiater: How would you describe your style as a director?

Romero: I haven't been able to define my style yet, and I think that in my mind I'm always experimenting. In every film that I make there are sequences in them that are different, where I'll try something new. I think I'm a stylist more than anything else. You can recognize Alfred Hitchcock's style the way you can recognize Bach, you know. He probably *is* the Bach of filmmakers! To me, Hitchcock wrote the textbook on suspense cinema. Everyone says that my style is a lot like Hitchcock's, and it's funny because I don't think it is. I think it's more like Orson Welles's, and I don't mean to elevate myself to that level. I'm not saying that I'm not good, but if there is anybody that I try consciously to emulate, it would be Orson Welles more than Hitchcock.

Wiater: Why Welles over Hitchcock, the acknowledged master of suspense?

Romero: I find it hard to watch Hitchcock movies. I find them slow, tedious, and yet they're great exercises. I enjoy watching them from an investigative point of view. But I never get involved with a Hitchcock character; they never bring a tear to my eye. So I find that his films are just not emotional in any way; they are very, very cold. My work, I think, is more emotional.

I can't tell you: "Here's a classic sequence." The only thing I can point to is humor. It's really hard for me to take things seriously sometimes and I can't resist a joke. So I will very often shuffle in humor, particularly with the shock material. Even if I went in with a vision, with something that was completely plotted out, I'd wind up just having to work within the budget. And to some extent, everybody does that. So it's rare when you have such control over the pages you have to get done that day, and the circumstances under which you have to do them allow you to shoot alternates or fool around. Or even just do what you planned in the first place.

Wiater: Some of your films have been quite explicit in their gore and violence. What kind of battles have you had over the years with the MPAA?

Romero: Personally, the rating system hasn't had a tremendous effect on me because all of the times that I did really graphic stuff, we had a distributor who was willing—and in fact wanted—to go out unrated. The only time I had to make physical cuts in something because of the MPAA was in *Martin*, and it only amounted to twelve frames across the course of the whole movie. I have had a lot worse problems overseas, and in other countries. In Ontario, I think they cut thirteen or seventeen minutes out of *Dawn of the Dead*, which is really major. It's all so gray and pliable. There are appeals to the ratings so if you have just made *All the President's Men* and you want someone to say "fuck," the MPAA will let you do it because you just made *All the President's Men* and not *Dawn of the Dead*. You can appeal, but those kinds of gray areas are always going to be there.

Wiater: Do you get the sense that the MPAA will always be prejudiced against horror movies, that they simply can't perceive them as worthy of any serious or artistic consideration?

Romero: There is a real prejudice by the *world*, I think.

Wiater: Please don't say it's always going to be "us against them."

Romero: I think so. There is definitely a prejudice against horror films. They are considered to be on the low totem, maybe one step up from chop-sockie movies, maybe not. Unless it's a major production, like *Aliens*, and the fact that the studio put $40 million into it, we are not supposed to take this genre seriously. I don't think people by and large in the mainstream take them very seriously.

Wiater: Recently a network news program did an interview with Roger Corman. To make a long story short, they presented Corman as if he was some kind of freak, making movies with crazy titles about ridiculous subjects, movies that the mainstream public were never supposed to have heard of before.

Romero: Sure! "Here's this curiosity." I've been there. I take my daughter to school, and someone will say, "Hey, I hear you make movies. What kind of movies do you make?" I'll say, "Well, horror movies, mostly." "Oh, I don't go to those." I mean, just flat, gone, no more interest! I probably would get more sparks if I was doing hard-core porn.

Wiater: The flip side of that, there are also people who love horror movies more than any other kind of film. Period. Doesn't that bring some kind of energy to your beleaguered creative soul?

Romero: You have to understand, there is a fandom, which is more dedicated probably than most other fandoms. But even that is sort of underground. Most people walking by the Sheraton when one of those horror conventions were on would probably steer a few blocks clear of it when they got a load of some of the people going in. Yet there are those rewards that come back because there is this incredibly dedicated fandom.

Wiater: Unlike perhaps any other genre, there are people who will faithfully line up to see a Cronenberg film or a Craven film or a Carpenter film or a Romero film. . . .

Romero: And it is true. I have a hard-core bunch of fans that will go see a beer commercial if I made it.

So it's rewarding in that way. There are times that you just wish that you could be one of the players. The people are saying, "How do you keep surviving? Why do you stay in Pittsburgh?," those kind of questions. Man, I'm making good money, people know who I am, I can call almost anyone in the business and at least get somebody's ear. But I don't want to play for bigger stakes. I like standing at the $2 window. I figure I can stand here longer.

Wiater: And not see your career halted by a major studio disaster?

Romero: Exactly! That has always been my philosophy, and I do much prefer it. My biggest frustration is I would like sometime to have a comfortable budget where I could just once say, "This is really exactly what I intended," just to see if there is a style and identify it.

Wiater: You've had books written about you, and there have been major retrospectives of your films. Any thoughts about where George Romero will eventually wind up in the history of the cinema?

Romero: I don't know. I think it might look something like that Roger Corman profile: "You might not know about this guy, but there was once this strange guy . . ." [Chuckle.] I'll be in the chapter about Earl Owensby and John Waters, if there is ever a definitive Britannica on this. At least I've earned that much. [Pauses.] I hope that someday one of my other films may buy me another inch of space in that book, and it doesn't just continue to remain to be for *Night of Living Dead*.

Wiater: But with twenty years of hindsight, do you have any major regrets about where your career has taken you?

Romero: No, I don't have a regret in the world. I'm doing exactly what I wanted to do, I've done it all my life. I've never had another job, I've never even had to wait a table. How can I be pissed off about anything?

Wiater: Yet some people in the horror business seem to be somehow embarrassed to be so closely associated with it. I can never understand how someone can first embrace a genre, and then, try to distance themselves from it after they become successful.

Romero: A lot of people are sensitive about it because it's one of those things that you don't want to admit. I can't think of a good analogy, but it's like having herpes and not wanting to say right away that you've got herpes.

Wiater: No, that's pretty apt—some critics contend that fans of this genre must be "sick" to enjoy it. Are you ever concerned that you might, in some small way, be bringing harm, not entertainment or art, to the public?

Romero: No. I've really looked for it, because I worry about it obviously. If you have a conscience, you examine it a lot. But I really don't believe that it's true. If the pop culture has contributed to the desensitization of America's youth, it does it in all sorts of insidious ways. And horror movies are only a part of it. As is rock 'n' roll. But also as is the National Football League and everything else—it's this barrage of advertising and electronic media. I think the lack of ethics, the breaking up of families, the destruction of the planet—all of those things are bigger factors. *That's* what makes you apathetic.

Wiater: Do you have an argument against those who feel that to display horror and gore in the movies serves no useful purpose in our society?

Romero: I still think most of the data indicates that, in fact, it acts as a defusing element, the same way that porn does. Based on the things that I've read about it, and the people that I've talked to about it, that's what I believe. Yeah, maybe I'm just building my own case, but that is what I believe. Fantasy is fantasy—it's no worse than dreams. If you read Joseph Campbell, he says we need this stuff, and I believe him, too. We need some kind of heroes, and I think that putting them in the context of another world is safer than *Beverly Hills Cop* for that matter.

Wiater: In other words, when in doubt about figuring out this world, shoot somebody?

Romero: Yeah, shoot somebody or put them through a plate glass window. Those actions are acceptable to these kids on the streets. You can behave that way, and you don't need a laser blaster or anything else. I'm very comfortable with my conscience; all the blood I've spilled has been spilled by zombies. Always in the fantasy context, except for *Martin*. In fact, *Martin* is about a kid who in my mind was affected by everything from the pop culture on. What I mean is, it's the only one of my movies where the central character is a human being doing violent things to other humans.

Wiater: Since you're considered one of the kings of independent filmmaking, what practical advice can you give to someone wishing to follow in your footsteps? That is, making movies without making the move automatically to Hollywood?

Romero: I always say the same thing: you have to get around a film production, somehow. The best way is to work your way through the ranks, unless you get real lucky like me and go make an independent movie and it becomes a hit. Then you'll get a blank check. So I'll never discourage anybody from going out and trying to make a little movie. That's cool.

But if you can't do that, if you don't have an uncle who will give you a couple of grand, you have to get around somebody else's production. That means getting to a city where there is state-of-the-art production activity. Now, that doesn't necessarily mean that they are making features, but somewhere there's an active PBS station, like Boston or Pittsburgh. Some place where you can meet the working professionals, get on the set, work for free if you have to, make relationships. That's exactly the way it works. It's all grapevine, and anyone who has the instinct and the talent and the dedication will come and find work.

It comes down to those old values. One thing about a film production is that it must run efficiently; there is no room for dead wood. So somebody that hangs around by the coffee wagon won't get hired again, but somebody who is dedicated and works hard and really puts out will get noticed by the people that matter around there, and will get asked to come back again. I've never seen it fail, it's almost automatic. If you have that spark, if you've got what it takes, you'll work.

It's as simple as that—there's nothing mysterious about it.

George Romero on *Bruiser,* Development Hell, and Other Sundry Matters

Dennis Fischer/1999

Previously unpublished interview. Printed with the permission of Dennis Fischer.

> The man had gone to market, to buy a diamond ring.
> The man who never noticed, that he was not a king.
> He chose the brightest sparkle, a diamond made of glass.
> The setting bright and gold, was crafted out of brass.
> The man spent all his money, the jeweler was a cheat.
> He told the man that royals, wore diamonds on their feet.
> The man went proudly walking, inside his shoe the ring.
> And no one ever told him, that he was not a king.
> —George A. Romero from *Bruiser*

When filmmaker Adam Simon put together a great documentary on American horror films called *The American Nightmare* (2000), I was assigned to cover it by the late Fred Clarke, editor of *Cinefantastique* magazine. I was also given the phone numbers of a couple of directors who had contributed commentary to the documentary, one of them being George Romero, to interview for a possible sidebar. The piece about Simon's excellent documentary was eventually published in the magazine, but not the sidebar interviews, which covered some rather interesting material.

I had interviewed Romero previously for *Cinefantastique* (regarding his work on *Monkey Shines*) as well as for my own book project, *Horror Film Directors*, published in 1991 by McFarland & Co. We spent some time commiserating over the sad state of independent cinema in the U.S.

Like the ever-ailing theater, independent cinema was undergoing its own new period of crisis as many of the independent distributors had overspent on faltering productions and gone out of business. I was interested in what Romero had been up to, as it had been a while since *The Dark Half* was released, and despite several projects being announced, including a remake of *The Mummy* through Universal and a film called *Before I Wake*, none had come to fruition. This long period of furious activity but no results is known in the film business as "development hell," and Romero had just spent a long stretch in that particular inferno.

The following interview took place in 1999, while Romero was seeking a distributor for his just completed project *Bruiser*, a film he both wrote and directed. Financing for the film was provided by Le Studio Canal+ and distribution was eventually handled by Lions Gate Entertainment. *Bruiser*, which was advertised as "From the Creator of *Night of the Living Dead*" and "Meet the new face of terror," wasn't so much released as escaped, never finding much of an audience in theaters.

Fischer: So how has been going, George? It's been a while since I've seen a new film from you.
Romero: Well, it's a lot tougher. There are no independent distributors. The studios, the traditional sources of money, all want to shoot for the moon. They want a $100 million winner or they don't want anything. I think that's why we get so much eye candy and so little investment.

Fischer: Certainly it's been shown that you can make a good, profitable horror film without a major budget.
Romero: Whether it's cost or effects or whatever, you can't even . . . *Blair Witch* didn't help in showing these executives that you can scare people without spending 100 million bucks. So I think that's been the biggest problem, and the disappearance of independent distributors and the inability [for them] to get screens. It's just much, much tougher for any kind of film.

Fischer: But some good, artistic independent films do get made.
Romero: People say there are all these artistic films coming out. Yeah, but they are coming out from proven brokers like Miramax, that's the Mouse [i.e. Disney], so there is very little inventive work coming out.

Fischer: What have you been working on most recently?
Romero: I just finished a film that I think might be my best film [*Bruis-*

er]. We're having a hard time finding effective distribution for it. It's not a studio type picture. It's hard for people to define it, they can't envision the poster. It's a psychological thriller rather than a horror film. I think the expectation of what might be coming from me was to just have a flat-out horror film, and it's a much more thoughtful film. It's just tough to put a handle on it.

Fischer: I'm sure with your track record, you'll be able to find a distributor.
Romero: I'm very confident that it will have a life. It's just really hard to get it out there in a meaningful way.

Fischer: So how did *Bruiser* come about?
Romero: It was a couple of years thinking about it. I think I was inspired by the film called *Eyes Without a Face* [aka Franju's *Horror Chamber of Dr. Faustus*]. I just loved the image of that blank face. I played around with several different ways of trying to do it, and decided that today the best way to do it would be with disenchantment—people's identity being taken away. That's the way I wound up deciding to go.

Fischer: What came next?
Romero: A lot of frustration. I've been working the whole time, but just not producing anything. We had a two-year deal at New Line. We had a three-year development project that went to two different studios. It's just been a nightmare. Hollywood development stuff, big stuff, you know, writing draft after draft to the point where you lost interest in it. Either that way or they don't like the direction you're going in. So I've decided to go back to the roots and do something smaller and more personal.

Fischer: Did you film it in Pittsburgh as usual?
Romero: It was an all-Canadian crew, a wonderful crew. It was shot in Toronto. They were really dedicated people. I mean they pulled it off 110 percent. It was fun and it was friendly. It was a wonderful, really enjoyable experience.

Fischer: Who's in it?
Romero: In the cast is a British actor, Jason Flemyng, who plays Henry Creedlow, Peter Stormare, whom you may know from *Armageddon* and

Fargo, Leslie Hope, and Nina Gabiras, who is sort of an up-and-comer from New York.

Fischer: And the story?

Romero: It's a guy who's been a good soldier all his life and just doing what he thinks people expect of him, and he winds up getting shit on so much that he comes to believe he has totally lost his identity—that's depicted by him basically losing his face. There's a reason near the beginning of the film that puts the image in his mind. A woman that he works with does life-masks, and she makes one of him. In an earlier scene, she asks him to paint it, do what he can so people will recognize that it is him. He has absolutely no idea.

So that image is what comes back to his mind when he believes he becomes faceless. I don't think he really is. I don't think it's a supernatural event; it's more like *Martin*, where it's probably in his head. All this disenfranchisement takes away his identity in his mind and frees him to go out and take revenge, to stand up for himself.

Fischer: How would you describe the look of the film?

Romero: It's a very fluid film, and it's very contemporary. It's very realistic. It's a bit like my old stuff—it's a little gaudier than, say, *Martin*. It's harder lighting, that very old-fashioned MGM quality to it, which is what I am going for. I was going for a heightened reality, something that depicts the emptiness of the world on the one hand, and on the other hand, a lot of clutter that is meaningless. It has a gothic kind of a look. I was trying to stick to those roots, too, but keep it contemporary.

Fischer: Why does Creedlow feel as if he has lost his identity?

Romero: Because of some of the people that are shitting on him, his boss, his wife. His wife is a real gold digger. She's driving him broke, she's actually stealing from their investment account with the aid of his best buddy, who is also his financial adviser. He's just such a wimp that everybody [walks all over him].

They treat him as if he is not there. His wife is very flat out about it. "You hear of women who screw their way to the top? I've been screwing my way to the bottom." She's just flat out about it, and so is his boss. They treat him like he's always good for a joke.

His boss runs a magazine, a bit like *Me* magazine, like *Styles*, a magazine my daughter reads. [The magazine's message is] "Look like this, be like this." It's not quite fashion, it's more like what's happening, what's in.

Fischer: Weren't you working on a Stephen King project recently?
Romero: *The Girl Who Loved Tom Gordon*. I just finished the script, and Steve likes it very much, and we're just waiting for paperwork on it. Hopefully, it's going to go down soon.

Fischer: Who's funding it?
Romero: Canal Plus.

Fischer: That would certainly be different than your prior King collaborations.
Romero: It's very different. That was one of things that blew me away. We were on a project called *Before I Wake* for about four-and-a-half years, first at MGM and then at Fox. They were gonna make it, they were insisting they were gonna make it. We actually had offices opened; the sets were designed, we were in casting and all that. But then they just started to stall, and we started to see the handwriting on the wall. We had literally twelve days to run on our exclusive contract with MGM, and in the meantime we'd been developing *The Mummy* at Universal, and they actually green-lit it. It was a go picture, and MGM wouldn't let us out. The two studios began to holler at each other, and MGM didn't make *Before I Wake* and we lost *The Mummy*. It was one of the most frustrating periods really, just made me want to quit.

Fischer: What is *Before I Wake*?
Romero: *Before I Wake* is a ghost story, which I still really love, but it's so tied up now with all the development costs from two different studios, it's got millions [charged] against it, even to go in and open the script would cost so much that its chances of getting made are pretty slim unless I suddenly get hot, you know, because of something. So I'm just kicking around doing the same old stuff, writing a couple of spec things, working with Steve on *Tom Gordon*.

Fischer: What happened between you and Laurel Productions?
Romero: We just didn't agree on an approach to running the company. My partner at the time, Richard Rubenstein, wanted to do more television and was more interested in the company as a public compa-

ny than in taking any risks. I've always wanted to be a feature guy, and I wanted to write my own stuff as much as possible, and I just wound up splitting. I still talk to him. I saw his brother, see him a lot, he did the score for *Bruiser*, so there's no bad blood. It was just a completely different idea about what way we wanted to go with our careers.

Fischer: I would have liked to have seen your take on *The Mummy*.
Romero: So would I. Well, it was very romantic. It was an unrequited love affair between Ankhesenamun and Imhotep. It was very, very romantic, very respectful of the original Karloff film, only with more action. It took place in a contemporary city at a museum, and it was just a very classic romance tale, the love that couldn't be with the same danger of him wanting to take her into death with him.

I loved it and they loved it. I mean, they green-lighted it, but it was very, very different [than the Steve Somers version]. It was like a $12 million movie as opposed to $100 million or whatever it was. I think it would have been great. I hated the [new] one when it first came out, when I first saw it, but I have a nine-year-old son and watching it through his eyes, I could really have fun with it now that it's sort of over. I think basically they are in much better shape with *The Mummy* that they have. They would have done maybe $40–$50 million with my version. I think it would have been scary, but I think that would have been its max if it hit.

Fischer: I understand that Universal was keen to make a version of *The Mummy* that didn't have any gore in it. Why do you think they were so keen to do a mummy movie?
Romero: I just think the mummy, the title and creature, has always had a tremendous appeal—it gets to people. I know people in my generation who watched the original *Mummy* and were scared shitless by it. So I think it has a draw. It's like a shark, and people are willing to suspend disbelief over it, 'cause there is so much in the real world about the curses of mummies. I had a lot more of that stuff in it. The lore and a lot of the history. There were times when people were eating mummies, thinking that it was some sort of snake oil.

I think it was scary, at least it was on the page. It probably would have been OK, but it certainly wasn't a big extravaganza by any stretch. It was "things that go bump in the night" in a museum.

Fischer: What did you think of that thirtieth-anniversary edition of

Night of the Living Dead that Jack Russo prepared and added scenes to?
Romero: I just had dinner with Jack this week, and I promised that I'm not going to go around badmouthing it. So the most I'll say is that I really don't like it. I understand why they did it—it's the same old thing, the copyright issue being all messed up. [Note: The original prints of *Night of the Living Dead* were sent out without a copyright notice on the prints, leading many to assume the film was in the public domain. Consequently, numerous copies of the film were sold for years without paying any royalties or residuals to the actual copyright holders.]

The company that owns *Night of the Living Dead*, the Pittsburgh company Image Ten, is like twenty-some investors that are all still alive, and there are only a couple of them that are still working at all in the business. It's their baby, so they keep trying to do things [to finally see a profit].

I really didn't want to do this. At first when they proposed it, it was just going to be dress it up, do a better mix, better sound effects, but what they wound up doing was replacing portions of it, which I just couldn't see doing that, and I didn't like the new material they replaced it with. I had nothing to do with it.

Fischer: Need I ask what you think of the colorized version of *Night* that was made?
Romero: I went along with the colorization. I went along with the remake. In fact, I participated in the remake [directed by Tom Savini from Romero's screenplay], writing it and everything.

Fischer: What did you think of the Elite restored edition of the original *Night*? I was impressed by the sharpness of the image after all those years of public domain prints.
Romero: Yeah, it looked a little too good. I thought it looked a little too flat or something, but I'm so used to looking at prints that were made on toilet paper.

Fischer: Elite also released a version of *Dawn of the Dead* that was advertised as a "Director's Cut." Which is your preferred cut of the film?
Romero: My preferred cut is the longest English-language cut that has a couple of Goblin pieces in it and a little bit of workprint. We couldn't get U.S. distribution, even though we had automatic European distribution, and so we made a print and that was it. We showed four-

walled, literally, that's how we got distribution. We rented a theater in New York and took an ad in the paper and said we were showing it, and a few distributors came and saw the audience reaction, and that's how UATC (United Artists Theater Chain) picked it up. That's the print, that's the version. They asked us to cut, but that's the version that's out there now. It had mostly library music and just a couple of Goblin cuts on it. There are some sections of it that are not very clear because they were printed off a workprint, but that's my favorite version. [Note: The so-called director's cut is the full workprint version and doesn't have any Goblin cuts in it.]

Fischer: While you are best-known for your zombie films, I like a lot of your other films as well, and was particularly impressed with *The Crazies* and *Knightriders*.
Romero: I liked *The Crazies*. We had no money on a lot of the real early stuff. *Jack's Wife* is a movie that I would like to remake. It's the only one I feel I would really like to remake, update it, do it nineties, but I haven't been able to convince anyone to go along with that.

Fischer: Fortunately, many of these other films have been discovered by people on video.
Romero: Oh sure. It's wonderful that your stuff can still be out there and be seen. It's been tremendous. This stuff just never goes away. I've been very lucky. My stuff seems to have a lot of shelf life. I feel really lucky that way. I can go out and speak or whatever, [and] people know the stuff because they are able to see it.

Fischer: Would you like to do another segment in the *Dead* series?
Romero: Yeah, I would. I wanted to do one for the nineties. I had this conceit that the first one is sixties, then seventies, then eighties, and I wanted to do the nineties, but we so were embroiled in all of this other stuff that I never got around to it. I'd like to.

Fischer: When you started, did you review the old zombie movies?
Romero: In the old stuff, all the traditional uses of zombies, they were just slaves. They were worker bees. They were just scary. They were slow and they were lumbering. They were scary just because they were dead things. I always felt they were the most descriptive of the monsters as us, sort of the way I went with it.

Fischer: Obviously, *Night of the Living Dead* is very much a film of its time.

Romero: Oh sure. That was in our minds the whole time. That's where it all came from. I mean the sixties is King and Kennedy and all that anger. That was always in our thinking. It's really in all three of the films, and although the third one is so much smaller [than I intended], the soldiers themselves trapped down there represent that mentality.

Fischer: It doesn't seem as if current horror films are doing that same kind of social commentary,

Romero: It's tough to find it in a lot of stuff they are looking at today. I think there is some, but I think there are very few films out there that provide it. I find our daughter and her friends go out and see the contemporary films, either comedies or dramas about people their age, that's more relative to them. There's nothing out there that sets you thinking. There are no parables and very little social criticism in any of the action or horror stuff that you see. It pretty much is what it is, just a flat-out rollercoaster ride.

Fischer: What themes are you interested in exploring?

Romero: I've always tried to work in a lot of the same things. I have characters who are not communicating, going along with an ideal, which speaks to the fanaticism or patriotism or whatever that causes war. I like to work with those themes, and pretty consistently throughout, if I can take a jab at the media or the church or the government, I can't let it go by.

Fischer: Will you be adding your themes to *Tom Gordon*?

Romero: There's a theme there, but I think her dad says it right. It's the sub-audible. It's a really nice story. I enjoyed reading it, and I think it can make a really nice, moody little film. I mean it's like the other times I've worked with Steve—when it's my stuff, I'm much more concerned about the underbelly—I'm concerned with executing it and doing what Steve intended.

Fischer: Will you ever make that much-talked-about movie version of *The Stand*?

Romero: I'd love to. I worked on it with Steve for quite a long time. At the time he didn't want to do it on TV, he thought it would be too restrictive, and he insisted that it would be three hours, and we just couldn't sell it to anybody. We did a lot of work on it. We worked together on the script for a long time. I'd love to do it. I don't know if it's something that can be remade, though Steve seems to do that on his own, so . . .

Fischer: So what do you think is the main difficulty in making good movies these days?

Romero: Anymore, it's just the producing mentality. It's very hard to find producers who have any affection for the medium. It's business all the way now, and it's just hard to sell a personal idea. Sundance, you can point to a few people. There are Oscar [bait] films or they will take a flyer on a young filmmaker, but a film like *Pi* is a rare bird. I just don't see a lot happening here in that way.

Fischer: Is there any place making particularly good movies?

Romero: In some of the European markets where there is less at stake, and they are not shooting for the 100 million bucks, you have some good work happening. There is also some very stilted work, I think.

Fischer: You said you really enjoyed working with the crew on *Bruiser*. Tell us about them.

Romero: D.P.'s name is Adam Swica, who is wonderful, just unbelievable. He made shots that I have never been able to make before, just really dedicated. We had a wonderful production designer, Sandy Kybartas, and a great editor, Miume Jan Eramo—all Canadian. Just a wonderful crew. It was a pleasure. It's the first time I've had a really good time on the set for years, probably since *Knightriders*.

Fischer: It always helps when everyone takes a personal interest.

Romero: We were all involved. Basically, we all became a troupe. We lived in one motel out there in the country, and we were fighting the weather. It was like *The Pride and the Passion*—we were all pulling that cannon, trying to get it over the hill. It was great.

Fischer: I was impressed with the acting, the scope, and the ambition of *Knightriders*. I'm sorry that it didn't make more of an impression in the marketplace.

Romero: We were all buddies, Ed [Harris] and I and Brother Blue—we were really a family. That was terrific. It had no distribution. I mean there was no advertising. You can't take a little film, put it in three or four theaters, and not do any buzz. It wasn't platformed that way. It wasn't carefully platformed, they just put it out. A lot of these distributions guys have the feeling that you're rolling the dice anyways, so just put it out and see what happens.

Fischer: *Monkey Shines* also wound up having some distribution problems, didn't it?

Romero: Orion put out twelve hundred prints and didn't support it with advertising, so who is going to see that one? No stars. It'd have to open on a rainy weekend and nothing against it at all. We were up against *Cocktail*, and all this other stuff. Unfortunately, they know. Movie opens on a Friday night, the first one o'clock show in New York means that by two o'clock in L.A. they know whether they have a hit or not. They can pull all their advertising and make all their decision right then. It's very unforgiving.

That's what killed *The Dark Half*. They didn't like *Dances with Wolves*. They didn't like *Silence of the Lambs*. They put all their marbles—those were the movies they were selling off—they liked *Mermaids*?! There is always that, the personal tastes of the people running the company. I think they could have a couple of really blockbuster tears with those hits, but they put all their marbles behind things like their productions like *Westies*, *Colors*, stuff like that. Those were the movies they thought pertinent. I mean I was there when they came out of the first screenings of *Silence of the Lambs*, saying, "Oy, who's going to see this?"

Fischer: You certainly made the point in *The American Nightmare* that talented filmmakers can use horror films to make comments about modern-day society.

Romero: I think damned near anything you want to say, you can say it in genre. It's much easier because you can be a little more obvious, you don't have to be quite as eloquent. You can make anything happen that you want to happen, so you can illustrate almost any point. I just think it's great. It's like parables, those little tales in the Bible. I think you could pick out anything, any scene that intrigued you or you felt passionate about, and figure out a way of telling it in a fantastic manner.

I think that plays a big part of it with a lot of stuff. But it's also a fun ride. My daughter and her buddies aren't going to go back and watch

American Beauty again, but they still watch the Freddy flicks. If there's one of those that somebody hasn't seen, they'll all sit around and try to scare that person. It has that part of it, too. It's got that ride aspect to it and that makes it fun.

Fischer: Anything else that you would like to add?
Romero: I just want to say I loved *The American Nightmare*. It's one of the best pieces I have ever seen.

An Interview with
George and Christine Romero

Tony Williams/2000

From *Quarterly Review of Film and Video* 18, no. 4 (2001): 397–411. Interview conducted on July 29, 2000. Reprinted by permission.

Tony Williams: When I visited Pittsburgh in 1992, Tony Buba told me about a fascinating scene from the original 204-page screenplay of *Day of the Dead*. He described a scene with helicopters playing "Amazing Grace" on their p.a. systems and zapping zombies. Was this really in the original version?

George Romero: I don't remember the use of "Amazing Grace." But I remember writing a scene about the helicopters attacking zombies in the city. The original was a bigger script and would have cost too much to film. They were willing to finance it but the difference was that this version would have cost $7 million and would have become an R-rated picture. I don't remember the "Amazing Grace" sequence. I'll have to go and look it up.

Tony Williams: Can you remember what other incidents appeared in the original draft of the *Day of the Dead* screenplay?

George Romero: It contained a lot of material involving the compound and the city of the dead. You see some remnants of this material in the opening of the existing print of the film. The compound was above ground and it was walled off. Many incidents appeared the other way around in the original. The humans captured the city. But my memory is terrible. Anyway, there were many differences. A lot more happened on both locations. But it just would have been too expensive to film. The principals were the same such as the doctor who was experimenting on the zombies to see if they had any germ of intelligence.

Characters such as Miguel and the Army guys remained the same. The original screenplay was much bigger in scope with more themes and characters involved.

Tony Williams: You've often mentioned that *Tales of Hoffmann* (1951) has been a major influence on you.

George Romero: It was the first film I got completely involved with. An aunt and uncle took me to see it in downtown Manhattan when it first played. And that was an event for me since I was about eleven at the time. The imagery just blew me away completely. I wanted to go and see a Tarzan movie but my aunt and uncle said, "No! Come and see a bit of culture here." So I thought I was missing out. But I really fell in love with the film. There used to be a television show in New York called *Million Dollar Movie*. They would show the same film twice a day on weekdays, three times on Saturday, and three-to-four times on Sunday. *Tales of Hoffmann* appeared on it one week. I missed the first couple of days because I wasn't aware that it was on. But the moment I found it was on, I watched virtually every telecast. This was before the days of video so, naturally, I couldn't tape it. Those were the days you had to rent 16mm prints of any film. Most cities of any size had rental services and you could rent a surprising number of films. So once I started to look at *Tales of Hoffmann* I realized how much stuff Michael Powell did in the camera. Powell was so innovative in his technique. But it was also transparent so I could see how he achieved certain effects such as his use of an overprint in the scene of the ballet dancer on the lily ponds. I was beginning to understand how adept a director can be.

But, aside from that, the imagery was superb. Robert Helpmann is the greatest Dracula that ever was. Those eyes were compelling. I was impressed by the way Powell shot Helpmann sweeping around in his cape and craning down over the balcony in the tavern. I felt the film was so unique compared to most of the things we were seeing in American cinema such as the westerns and other dreadful stuff I used to watch. *Tales of Hoffmann* just took me into another world in terms of its innovative cinematic technique. So it really got me going.

Tony Williams: A really beautiful print exists on laserdisc with commentary by Martin Scorsese and others.

George Romero: I was invited to collaborate on the commentary by Marty. Pat Buba (Tony's brother) knew Thelma Schoonmaker and I got to meet Powell in later years. We had a wonderful dinner with him one evening. What an amazing guy! Eventually I got to see more of his movies that I'd never seen before such as *I Know Where I'm Going* and *A Canterbury Tale*. Anyway, I couldn't do the commentary on *Tales of Hoffmann* with Marty. But, back in the old days in New York, Marty and I were the only two people who would rent a 16mm copy of the film. Every time I found it was out I knew that he had it and each time he wanted it he knew who had it! So that made us buddies.

Tony Williams: In your 1997 interview with Norman England you mentioned you read Henry James as well as Edgar Allan Poe and H. P. Lovecraft. Were you serious here?

George Romero: Oh, yeah. For a time I read Henry James before I got silly! (laughter) I did write a screenplay for *Turn of the Screw* and I'd like to do it.

Tony Williams: I note some interesting parallels between James and some of your films where characters often engage in denial and self-deception. When did you start reading him?

George Romero: In my junior and senior years of high school and throughout college. I haven't been doing much reading since I've been out trying to make a buck. But I loved working on the *Turn of the Screw* screenplay with Michael Hirst. We really got to tear the book apart and start thinking deeply about it. When he was at Columbia David Puttnam got the project going. But you don't think about literary influences consciously in film because it's a parasitic medium. You don't consciously steal or plagiarize someone else's work or even imitate it unless you are specifically out to do so like DePalma who sets out to copy Hitchcock. But I don't. It's hard to pinpoint where any of the literary influences come from. It's probably a weird combination of James, comic books, Kerouac, Keaton, and Vonnegut. Let's put Vonnegut in there!

Tony Williams: Have you read any of the novels associated with the naturalist tradition such as those by Emile Zola, Theodore Dreiser, and Frank Norris.

George Romero: No.

Tony Williams: I mention that last two because Stephen King has mentioned that they influenced him while he was in college.

George Romero: No. I've never read any of them.

Tony Williams: During two interviews you did for *Andy Warhol's Interview* in 1969 and 1973 you mention that you envisaged *There's Always Vanilla* as dealing with the hippie generation five years later. Do you feel the film achieved this purpose?

George Romero: I don't think so. It wasn't my script. The writer and I were constantly having problems. I just think that the film was a little frothy. It wasn't accomplished enough for my taste.

Tony Williams: After disappearing from circulation for many years, it is now back in distribution. Why did you allow it back into circulation?

George Romero: I have no objection to anyone seeing it. But I didn't think it would be worth anyone's while to watch it. Of course, now the video movement is just exploding you can sell anything. I don't mind it being available. I don't think it's bad. I shouldn't say that—I do! But I don't think it's terribly well made given the money we had. As I said, it's a little too frothy, very loose, and didn't really explore what it's meant to explore. For example, the jazz session in the beginning is very stiff. I never thought the film was successful even when I was working on it.

Tony Williams: Didn't the problems on this film lead to the break-up of friendships you had with people involved on *Night of the Living Dead* such as Russell Streiner and John Russo?

George Romero: Yeah, it did. But I still see all of those guys, even the writer. The guy who wrote it is probably my oldest friend in Pittsburgh. I met him in line when we enrolled as freshmen in college. His surname had the same initial as mine—Ricci and Romero. We still see each other. However, it wasn't any hideous break-up. It was more philosophical than anything.

Tony Williams: I notice in my video copy that you and Russell appear briefly in certain scenes of the film.

George Romero: I think maybe I appeared as a bartender. I don't remember.

Tony Williams: Isn't there a studio shot where your name and Russell's appear separately on slates and you both briefly appear directing?

George Romero: Maybe. I'll have to look at the film again.

Tony Williams: Is the audience really supposed to believe Ray Laine's version of "The Affair" in *There's Only Vanilla*?

George Romero: I was hoping for a *Rashomon* type of thing. But we never did achieve this. I was hoping to film an opposing perspective but we never got around to it.

Tony Williams: I don't mean to shock you but the more I look at it the more I think you achieved what you set out to do. I'd like to ask you another specific question concerning *The Crazies*. You never explain why David never becomes infected in the film. We never see him drinking the water like the other victims. But doesn't his survival have much to do with his rejection of the macho values represented by Clank?

George Romero: It's so hard to go all the way back to the time I made the film. You just get into new characters and situations with every film. But I don't think that I ever think as deeply as you do. So much of filmmaking is just instinctive or part of the decisions you make along the way. And then you forget about them the next day. I have absolutely no recollection of the reasons motivating this character. I'd have to go back and look at the film again. This is similar to the question you asked last night about the use of the lap dissolves in *Monkey Shines*. These are either instinctive or post-production decisions. I write technical terms on screenplays but it's often to make it a better read, to make sure that the reader knows that time is passing or we're moving on to another scene. We don't make these types of interpretative decisions when we're editing.

Tony Williams: *The Crazies* contains one really interesting scene between David and Judy when he tells her about rejecting violence. His head is in sharp focus in the foreground while his rifle is in soft focus in the background. He then pushes the rifle out of the frame. This seemed a really great visual metaphor for his feelings at this point of the film. But, again, it might just come down to the choice of lens and focus.

George Romero: I often pull the focus around a lot so I don't have to shoot in a lower light.

Tony Williams: Why did you choose a very abrupt editing style for *The Crazies*?

George Romero: We didn't have enough footage! (laughs) But I always felt that something worked out about that such as the graphic nature of that type of situation. It was a gamble. We didn't have enough footage because we either could not finish the film or it rained when I wanted to shoot. So what often happens in that type of situation is that you have to leave something behind and you can't glue it in anywhere. I decided that if I wanted to go a little nuts with the editing then I could do it. Then I found the drum music from the sound library and that provided a staccato rhythm. It helped the editing contribute to the film's nerve-wracking feeling.

Christine Romero: Yes, the first time I saw *The Crazies* I felt it was so jarring.

Tony Williams: Both you and Stephen King have mentioned the influence of EC Comics on your work. Would you like to explain how you have used this in your films?

George Romero: The influence is not so much visual. The irreverence and the graphic nature of those comics attracted me to them. I thought it was just part of the horror genre. It should be that way and nothing less. Everything stops a little short of doing it. It was really that.

Tony Williams: I notice that EC Comics have many poetic justice motifs. William Gaines published certain stories that were anti-lynching, which obviously caused him problems. Many of his war comics take issue with demonizing the Koreans in the Korean War and present that conflict in a very grim way.

George Romero: What I took from EC Comics was not so much that or, even, the poetic justice motifs—although I like to work with that idea a lot. But Steve and I have never discussed our interest in EC Comics in much detail though I'm sure he would say the same thing as me. The irreverence and uninhibited presentation influences him. But he also deals with poetic justice in his novels as well as random events affecting his characters. Last year, a random event happened to him when he was nearly killed by a vehicle.

Tony Williams: In *Night*, *Dawn*, and *The Crazies*, you hold the media responsible for abdicating responsibility and contributing to chaos.

George Romero: Yes, I do this in a very overt way. Generally, media behavior is atrocious. But I make this criticism more as an illustration in certain films rather than aiming at anything specific. But I do think the media has a tendency to exacerbate situations. I don't know whether they would put false rescue stations on the air when zombies attack. (pause) But, I don't know, they might.

Tony Williams: Your films contain many critiques of the talk-show phenomenon as in *Vanilla, Dawn*, your screenplay for Savini's version of *Night*, as well as your teleplay "The Devil's Advocate" in *Tales of the Darkside*. Dean Burbage in *Monkey Shines* is also a frequent guest on talk shows. What infuriates you most about this aspect of everyday life?

George Romero: Don't forget *Martin*. You'll also see this motif in *Bruiser*. I think the phenomenon is ridiculous. I use that stuff as wallpaper even when I'm writing. It provides a really interesting look at the way people behave or allow themselves to behave. I find that this talk-show stuff is either completely exploitative or you have people there who represent two sides of the same coin. You don't get any real information out of these shows at all.

Tony Williams: In *Dawn*, the TV station eventually turns into a very low-grade type of talk show with people screaming at each other and not getting anywhere.

George Romero: That's right—"not getting anywhere." You see any person on those shows with actually no information at all or knowing nothing about the condition they're discussing. It's amazing how they have these politicians on a talk show like *Crossfire* and they scream at each other. That's all you have to do defend your point of view just by saying, "No. That's not the way it was."

Christine Romero: I think that some people tune in to see and think that "my life's better than this!"

Tony Williams: When asked about a zombie movie for the nineties you've often mentioned the idea of "ignoring the problem." But many of your characters act the same way such as Chris in *Vanilla*, Joan Mitchell in *Jack's Wife*, Martin and Cuda in *Martin*, and Allan in *Monkey Shines*. They often choose to escape into their own particular fantasies and find convenient scapegoats rather than deal with the real issues affecting their lives.

George Romero: This is more of a societal phenomenon rather than an individual perception. This is all to the advantage of the authorities. They like watching the whole thing. That's what the nineties was all about—ignoring the problem. And it still happens.

Christine Romero: You're always talking about why doesn't someone change this or deal with it.

George Romero: There are really a few important questions that we'd like to answer and we ought to be able to get to them and try to answer them or study them. What's the point of just going to church every Sunday? In our neighborhood we live near this very high-faluting Presbyterian church and I don't think there's any sort of mystical thought going through anybody's head. They're all out there looking at each other and seeing how they're dressed and doing what they need to do to get into heaven by showing up for one hour every Sunday. It's American since it's all about money. Money directs where the research goes. It drives me nuts.

Christine Romero: What I can't figure out is the older I get the worse it all seems.

George Romero: I think the media is making it easier to ignore the problem. In other words, basically, you can put up two debaters and the "best" debater is going to win in the eyes of the public. They are going to support the person who says the right things and, unfortunately, more often than not that's not going to be the brightest guy or the one with any real answers. That person usually comes off as either grating or arrogant.

Tony Williams: I love the comparison you made in the *Dawn of the Dead* screenplay relating the mall to a cathedral.

George Romero: I really liked the idea. I don't know how I did it.

Tony Williams: Chris was a really great faculty wife in "The Crate" episode of *Creepshow*. Did your friends Cletus and Barbara Anderson provide you with information about academia?

George Romero: They're our best friends so we hang around with them a lot and hear all of their horror stories! We also meet a lot of these people at their parties. Fritz Weaver was great in his role. But he's doing all these voice-over narratives now. There aren't all that many great actors of his caliber in that age group around today.

Christine Romero: It's hard to find work now.

Tony Williams: I found "The Crate" really interesting in terms of revealing the deceptions and denials in academia. Although Adrienne Barbeau's Billie is irritating, she is also a human being. The Weaver and

Holbrook characters actually conspire to bring about her death and then deny it.

George Romero: Yes. Both Weaver and Holbrook decided to play their relationship in a very homosexual type of manner.

Tony Williams: What is the old movie Jordy Verrill watches on television in *Creepshow*?

George Romero: The original version of *A Star Is Born*.

Tony Williams: Do you ever intend to release your early seventies short documentary- fantasy *The Amusement Park* which deals with the plight of senior citizens in America? I refer to the film in the conclusion to my manuscript on your work.

George Romero: I haven't seen it for years.

Tony Williams: It would be great to add it as a supplement to any future DVD/ video release of your films.

George Romero: I've been thinking of doing that with some of my early short films. Lincoln Maazel, the father of conductor Lorin Maazel, worked with us on *The Amusement Park*. He also plays Cuda in *Martin*. Lincoln Maazel gave up a good life to come to Pittsburgh. He became a wonderful teacher. Now, there's a story.

Tony Williams: Some of your films often appear to blur the boundaries between fantasy and reality so it often becomes difficult to divide them. It is, sometimes, possible to do this in *Vanilla* and *Jack's Wife* but really difficult in *Martin* and *Day*. The prologue and epilogue of *Day* represents one particular example.

George Romero: In my mind, this is a device. I like taking someone along a certain track and then, all of a sudden, something happens. That's really the way I look at it. It's just a device to get your mind going on two planes rather than keeping it on a single track. You make an early interpretation of what the audience is watching and then change it for the rest of the presentation. I like playing around with that. You'll see a lot of this technique in *Bruiser*. I think, perhaps, that a lot of the events in the film really go on in the central character's head. The film is very similar to *Martin*. The basic idea is, what's in this guy's head and what's in the heads of the people who have molded him into what he's become? *Bruiser* is also a film about disenfranchisement. There's so much of that about now leading to the kind of frustration that turns into rage and violence. I think that's what Columbine's about, too. I got the idea of a man losing his face from Georges Franju's *Eyes Without a Face* (1959).

Tony Williams: *Day* begins with Sarah's nightmare of the hands breaking through the wall and reaching out to her. Was this inspired by Val Lewton's *Bedlam* (1945) or Roman Polanski's *Repulsion* (1966)?
George Romero: It was more of *Repulsion*.

Tony Williams: A zombie's hand reaches out to grab her towards the climax when she rushes towards the helicopter. Then an abrupt cut leads to her waking up on the desert island. We don't really know whether she has escaped or the island epilogue represents her last vision before death.
George Romero: It doesn't really matter.

Tony Williams: This is really similar to people asking what happened to Fran and Peter after the end of *Dawn* and you've replied, "They ran out of fuel and landed in Cleveland, Ohio." The new edition of *Night of the Living Dead* supplies the reason why the body is at the top of the stairs in the farmhouse. But who cares?
George Romero: A lot of people do!

Tony Williams: I saw the new edition on sale at a local video store and the manager told me that people who were excited about the extra footage returned later and asked if they could get their money back. Obviously, a thirty year difference exists between the way Bill Heinzeman originally looked in 1968 and his present appearance. A still on the video box cover reveals this discrepancy. No make-up in the world could make him look the way he was thirty years ago.
George Romero: Yes, it's impossible, absurd, and very clumsily done. I told Jack (Russo) that I'm not going to go on a rampage about this new version. I also mentioned this to Jay Douglas of Anchor Bay Video who is a very good friend. So I don't want to go on a crusade against the new edition and start screaming about it. But it is very frustrating that people don't read the information on the video box cover. So they think I had something to do with it. Chris and I saw it. Jack invited us to his office once they finished it. He was disappointed at the way we reacted. We didn't get into a fight but we had an argument about it.

Tony Williams: You've mentioned elsewhere that you are disappoint-ed with the new type of horror film and the lack of film history on the part of youthful audiences. I remember Paul Fussell, author of *The Great War and Modern Memory* and *Wartime*, telling me that he didn't think today's college students were all that different from their predecessors thirty or forty years ago. They don't know their own film culture. The old question of forty years ago, "Who the hell is Howards Hawks?" is more true today than it ever has been. Has Hawks been a great influ-ence on your work?

George Romero: I can't really say who I steal from! (laughs) But I loved all his films and all of those guys who worked in the old Hol-lywood system. When I was young that's what we watched in the the-aters so I got to see all that stuff first time out on a big screen. It was a big event in those days and really meant something such as seeing *Red River* (1948), with John Wayne, for the first time. Once in a while when I can't think of something to watch I put it on as I did the other night. I just love that movie. There are always certain styles that influence me or particular shots. But, honestly, you have no idea where this par-ticular shot comes from. You really have no idea so I'm sure something came from somebody's movie into mine. (laughs)

Tony Williams: Michael Powell once mentioned to me that "we all borrow from one another." He stated that Scorsese borrowed lighting techniques from his works. But most of this is unconscious and indirect as you say.

George Romero: I think most films do this. You can feel when the borrowing is intentional because it's very distinct and usually very ac-curate. Marty does that a lot. I guess it's because of Thelma (Schoon-maker) being his editor. Some of that stuff from *The Archers* is definitely "stolen." Are you running *The Life and Death of Colonel Blimp* (1942) in your classes?

Tony Williams: It depends whether I get a 400 or 500 level class and whether the students have the stamina to sit through a long film. But it is one of my favorite Powell films.

George Romero: It's unbelievable! I put it on one night and my daughter, Tina, walked into the room. She thought it was something by Spielberg in terms of the way it looked. But it's difficult to get any young person to sit down and watch that type of film over a period of time. It's due to the influence of MTV and the type of scattered images you see on album jackets. These influences don't allow for the reverence of that type of film that does not involve wit or satire but a particular type of irreverence.

Tony Williams: Have you seen many examples of Hong Kong Cinema?

George Romero: I really would like to have some more time to get into that type of stuff. I've only seen a few but found them all amazing.

Tony Williams: Was Howard Hawks's *Hatari!* (1961) influential on *Knightriders* (1981)?

George Romero: I don't know. That's an interesting question. I'm probably one of the few people in the world who still watch *Hatari!* Maybe, I borrowed some of those tracking shots involving the noose and other imagery. I don't know. Maybe, it had something to do with me getting the idea for *Knightriders*. But I don't think, directly, in terms of any visual transfer. I've always wanted to make a film in Africa and always felt that if I ever had a film I wanted to make there it would be *Tarzan*. It would be a purely straight adaptation of the Edgar Rice Burroughs novel purely in gratitude for his writing those twenty-seven books I read when I was growing up. I still would love to do it. It was well-researched. I was trying to sell it on the basis of a *Jaws* type of thing but that's not what it was about. It was a really well-made screenplay about problems in Africa such as poaching and environmental issues. It contained wonderful sequences such as dealing with when elephants die and their mating screaming. They're fascinating creatures. I'd still love to do something in Africa such as an up-to-date remake of *Something of Value* (1957) which originally dealt with the Mau Mau uprising against British rule in Kenya.

Christine Romero: You should try to resurrect that old screenplay you wrote once. It had a lot of elephants in it. George did a fabulous screenplay full of background details.

Tony Williams: You've elsewhere described *Knightriders* as being less about the problems facing The Latent Image in Pittsburgh and more about a Camelot ideal.

George Romero: Yes, definitely. I wasn't necessarily thinking about the film business. But, even then, there were studios and producers who would only hire directors who would only go along with their way of thinking. (laughter)

Tony Williams: *Knightriders* is a very beautiful and idealistic film and touching in many scenes.

George Romero: When we did the audio-commentary track for the Anchor Bay DVD version, we all had tears in our eyes at the end of the coronation scene. Tom (Savini) does the scene so beautifully. The musicians were actually there playing their music live when we were shooting it.

Christine Romero: You couldn't shoot a movie like that anymore. It was so beautiful. Today's motion picture executives would never let George shoot a movie like that today.

George Romero: They would have wanted a more structured . . . not structured because *Knightriders* has a pretty tight structure, but something with a clear-cut premise which is more scary and less ambiguous all the way. It was the first time I made a film in thirty days just like *Bruiser*, which was shot in Canada. I find the crews up there just phenomenal. It was so great to work with people who cared about the film such as the set designer who would often say, "I don't think this character would have this ash tray" and then supply the right one. It was wonderful to have that amount of collaborative spirit. I worked with a great d.p. (director of photography) who did shots I had hoped to make on other productions with bigger d.p.'s such as Tony Pierce-Roberts on *The Dark Half* (1991). He'd say, "That's it! Two shots for this morning."

Tony Williams: What was your original ending for *Monkey Shines* going to be?

George Romero: Allan would not recover as in Michael Stewart's original novel. Also, the final scene would show Dean Burbage (who disappears half-way from the version now in circulation) trying to find out more information in the laboratory. My idea of a shock ending was that a monkey would land on his shoulder. But after some previews, Orion insisted on a happy ending as well as the *Carrie* imitation when Allan undergoes his surgery. But after some other previews, audiences complained about the happy ending the studio imposed! Orion went ahead anyway.

Tony Williams: Stewart's novel mentions the masochistic tendencies in Allan's character. You never spell this out in the screenplay or film.

But it is definitely there in Jason Beghe's performance. Your direction of actors is so subtle in the film. One great performance is by Joyce Van Patten as Allan's mother.

George Romero: I thought she was great too. But everyone thought she was over the top!

Tony Williams: In your contribution to *Two Evil Eyes* (1990)—"The Facts in the Case of Mr. Valdemar"—you use the triangular design on the American dollar bill as a murderous implement. As you see, from this dollar bill I'm showing you, the triangle has an eye so this must be your "one evil eye." The metronome that penetrates Hoffman is triangular, as is the building seen outside his apartment after the janitor calls the detectives.

George Romero: That was a real building.

Tony Williams: Was it your idea to change the sex of Thad's faculty mentor in *The Dark Half* (1991) to Julie Harris's Reggie De Lesseps?

George Romero: Yes. It was my idea but it really came out of not being able to find a male cameo performer. We were running around at the time and couldn't get anyone. So I suggested changing the character's gender. Steve (King) went along with it. I think it works out great and I'm much happier with it.

Tony Williams: The change relates Reggie to your other aware female characters such as Fran in *Dawn* and Sarah in *Day*.

George Romero: Again, this may not have been directly in my mind. I'm always trying to put women in challenging roles. But it's a tough sell particularly in Hollywood projects. They still have the same prejudices about female leads, black leads, and Asian leads. It's unbelievable. A lot of ageism exists there. They don't believe I can make a film for young people because of my age!

Tony Williams: In *The Dark Half*, the "diaper duty" sequence is not in the book. I'm wondering whether you wrote this to contrast Jack Torrance's attitude in King's novel *The Shining*. Jack becomes enraged when he finds Danny interfering with his work. By contrast, Thad's attitude to his child tearing up his pages is that he is a "born editor."

George Romero: No, it wasn't. At least, not consciously.

Tony Williams: Thad's wife was played by Amy Madigan who is married to Ed Harris who gave some great performances in two of your films.

George Romero: He's wonderful. I wish we could do something together again. We've tried a couple of times, but . . .

Tony Williams: Did you add the Elvis twin motif from John Carpenter's *Elvis* (1979) TV movie? The use of "Are You Lonesome Tonight" was really powerful.

George Romero: We were experimenting with how Stark should look in the film. So we started to mess around with the hair and got an Elvis look. But it wasn't until I began editing that I found the song. What I originally wanted to do was have a big gag at the end by using "Return to Sender"!

Tony Williams: King's novel never really describes Stark's appearance so you filled in his character very well.

George Romero: Yes. I'm really proud of that too. A lot of it was due to Timothy Hutton. He and I got into hot water half way through the film, but after that we were really able to work well together. By the end of the film I really appreciated his performance which I thought was great.

Tony Williams: In your screenplay for Tom Savini's version of *Night of the Living Dead* (1990) did you mean to suggest that the new version of Barbara is in danger of being contaminated by the male violence she watches at the climax? She also engaged in violence herself during the film.

George Romero: Yes. Well, my idea was that all along she's becoming a guy! She's almost half way there when you first meet her. I was trying a little of that with Sarah in *Day*. But Lori Cardille didn't quite get there. We talked about it a couple of times and she tried to do it. But it didn't work. Patty (Tallman) is a stunt woman. That's her trade.

Tony Williams: Between *The Dark Half* and *Bruiser* you've frequently referred to the problems of being in "development hell." What has happened to the *Resident Evil* project?

George Romero: I don't know if you've heard of a company called Constantine. I think that we were doing a really good job of getting the

Resident Evil project into shape. I loved the script. It was perfectly in character with the game and wasn't an embarrassment. I tried to insert some of my usual humor and socio-political satire into it. I thought it would be great to go back and do a zombie thing without it having the burden of being on the same track as my other films. But when we returned early from our holiday in Mexico and expected the project to get the green light, the producer told us at dinner, "I can't make something like this!"

Christine Romero: They never kept in touch with George and only paid him for one or two drafts when he'd written seven or eight.
George Romero: It's terrible. I know the Writer's Guild is trying to crack down on this. But when you turn in your first draft, theoretically, you are supposed to get conclusion money. Then they give you this story about re-submission. Basically, they're asking you to do polishing work—in some cases, elaborate polishing before they even say it's a first draft. It's just horrible. The other thing is that they will send a project out to four or five people. But they won't phone and ask you to send them a twenty-minute thesis of how you might approach it. They want you to write a treatment but they won't pay you for treatments. It's ludicrous. They're getting away with murder.

Tony Williams: I believe you were also working on Universal's remake of *The Mummy* at one time.
George Romero: I was also working on a project called *Before I Wake* for MGM which they kept telling us they were going to shoot. Then Universal gave me the green light on *The Mummy* script. But because I got trapped into *Before I Wake*, which they never shot, I could not get out of the MGM contract. So I never directed *The Mummy*.

Tony Williams: I have to ask the question you're most dreading. Do you still intend to make that concluding chapter to your trilogy, *Twilight of the Dead*?
George Romero: I'd love to do it and I'm looking for a way to begin doing it. But what I need to do is find a fresh way to approach the subject. I can't really make it as a continuation of the other films. None of them have continuing characters anyway although they treat the same phenomenon. I think I need to find a way to think of a fresh treatment rather than having to do a lot of "pilot pitch."

Tony Williams: Did you write some screenplays in the past to help your associates Tom Savini, Michael Gornick, and John Harrison obtain director credits?

George Romero: Yes. Mike directed *Creepshow 2* while Tom did the 1990 version of *Night of the Living Dead* as well as some of the *Tales of the Darkside* television episodes.

Tony Williams: Has Orson Welles been influential on your work?

George Romero: Definitely, in the visual sense. When I was shooting my own films I often looked through the camera and tried to see how Welles would compose a shot. I love all of his films. As a filmmaker, he really directs your eye with the things he plays with in the frame. For example, in the opening shot of *Touch of Evil*, the camera cranes over the street and shows all the women and revelers. It's just such a great image, which perfectly defines his talent. I haven't seen the new version though. I've heard they removed the Henry Mancini score.

Tony Williams: John Harrison's "The Cat from Hell" episode of *Tales from the Darkside: The Movie* contains several laps dissolves reminiscent of scenes in *Citizen Kane* when a character such as Jed Leland begins to remember the past. Was this in your original screenplay?

George Romero: No, that was John. I didn't have any reference to that in my screenplay. John's doing *Dune* in Hollywood now. He's also done a bunch of things for television and received a credit as head writer on *Dinosaur*.

Tony Williams: Which one of your films would you like to remake today?

George Romero: *Jack's Wife*. I think it would be more pertinent today than it was when I first shot it.

Tony Williams: What types of films interest you today?

George Romero: I like John Sayles's work and the Coen Brothers stuff. But I haven't seen a good horror film since the first *Candyman*.

Tony Williams: You've preferred to live in Pittsburgh rather than Hollywood. What attracts you to the area?

George Romero: I have a lot of friends in Pittsburgh and there is less static there unlike Hollywood. Everyone talks movies in LA, and making pitches is very similar to doing penance. I'm not interested in doing penance.

Tony Williams: What are your plans for the future?

George Romero: I'm working on an adaptation of Stephen King's *The Girl Who Loved Tom Gordon* which is very near to completion and *The Ill* screenplay. Also, I'm collaborating with Tom Savini on an adaptation of *Macbeth* for the Pittsburgh Playhouse next year.

Let Them Eat Flesh

Giulia D'Agnolo-Vallan/2005

From *Film Comment* 41, no. 4 (2005): 23–24. Reprinted by permission.

Twenty years have passed since we left Sarah and John, the protagonists of *Day of the Dead*, on a sunny, deserted island—a quiet image of hope for a new beginning for humanity, before *Survivor* spoiled that notion forever.

All is darkness in *Land of the Dead,* the new chapter in George A. Romero's living-dead saga, which unfolds in a hellish, seemingly endless night. "EAT," commands the broken electric sign of an abandoned diner at the beginning of the film—immediately reminding us of Romero's ferocious sense of humor. With a gentle, almost loving touch (in one of those subtle trademark camera moves that friend John Carpenter says makes Romero such a great filmmaker), his lens caresses the lost, mournfully soulless face of a solitary zombie woman, before revealing a large mob of the aimless undead standing around.

In the Pittsburgh filmmaker's deeply fascinating, often troubled filmography, it is movies like *Martin* and (especially) *Knightriders* that he considers "close to my heart." Yet the *Dead* cycle—the fulgurating black and white of *Night of the Living Dead* (1968), the bloody comic-book humor of *Dawn of the Dead* (1978), the radical nihilism of *Day of the Dead* (1985)—represents something as personal, obsessive, and fundamental to his oeuvre as *Star Wars* is to that of George Lucas. It is, in Romero's words, "the place where I can show most how I see the world. My own way of saying, 'Hey guys, here I am, and this is what I am thinking!' The political dimension of these films is what's important to me. They may not be 'political' films like Michael Moore's . . . but I don't think I am going to be invited to the White House anytime soon."

Land of the Dead, whose screenplay Romero completed shortly before 9/11, shelved for a couple of years, and then reworked a little more, is no exception. Like his preceding zombie films, it is firmly rooted in its time, defining an epoch.

Shot in Toronto but set in Pittsburgh, the city between two rivers ("America always felt protected by water, and they still do, even if a few guys obviously got across," says the director), *Land* takes place in a society where the rich and powerful—led by technocrat Kaufman (Dennis Hopper)—inhabit Fiddler's Green, a lavish high-rise that's a shinier, Trump-like version of *Dawn*'s shopping mall. It is surrounded by a riverbank ghetto—a dark, miserable encampment of disenfranchised shadows. Across the water: the land of the dead.

"I tried to set up a little depiction of what America is like today," Romero told me in Cannes, where a twenty-minute preview of *Land* received a gigantic standing ovation. "Maybe it is a little jazzy, a little interpretative, but in a certain way it represents what is going on."

A paramilitary group led by Riley (Simon Baker) and Cholo (John Leguizamo), and later joined by Slack (Asia Argento), are paid by the elite to bring in supplies from the outside world—a risky proposition as the expeditions involve foraging in the midst of the cannibalistic ghouls. While the living patrol the night searching for luxury goods left over from what feels like another age, the zombies are kept at bay with . . . fireworks. Mesmerized, the living dead stare up, transfixed by the bright colored lights in the night sky—a simple, effective reminder of our own ready-to-be-lobotomized minds. These zombies will never run as they did in last year's *Dawn of the Dead* remake ("Before going to the gym my guys will go to the library," laughs Romero, who didn't dislike Zack Snyder's reworking but thought "it completely lost its reason for being"), but they have evolved considerably since 1968, when he borrowed the premise of Richard Matheson's novel *I Am Legend* and replaced its post-apocalyptic vampires with his "blue-collar monsters." In the new film, the army of the dead takes to the road and, led by a towering gas-station attendant nicknamed Big Daddy, heads for the glimmering high-rise.

"In my mind, the zombies have always been evolving," says Romero, explaining the progression of his films. "Even in *Dawn* I was trying to show some zombies with 'personalities'—a softball player, a nun . . . that poor guy on the escalator, just trying to get by. I was trying to give them some sympathy. And at the very end, when Peter is escaping and a zombie grabs his gun, he makes a decision that it is a better gun than the one he has. In other words, I have tried to make them progress. Bub [the slightly "domesticated" zombie in *Day of the Dead*] to me is classic Karloff, a sympathetic monster. This time, in *Land*, they are a little more organized. Big Daddy is not instantly as sympathetic as Bub. He is . . . [a figure like] Zapata."

"You see," he adds, "I have always felt less attraction for the humans. I may have a protagonist who is thinking a bit more clearly than all the others, but the humans have always been less sympathetic to me."

Despite its in-your-face politics, as radical and explicit as they were in all of the series' previous installments, *Land of the Dead* is the most expensive of Romero's zombie films—reportedly $18 million, not much by today's standards but a long way from *Night*'s $115,000 and *Day*'s $3 million. Not surprisingly, it has a more polished look than its predecessors, and bigger action scenes, although what stays with you most is the film's profound sadness, an almost lyrical quality, and the impenetrable darkness that surrounds everything. Likely made possible by the box-office success of *Dawn*'s remake, the *Resident Evil* films, and horror movies like *The Grudge*, *Land of the Dead* couldn't be more different. "I could never dream up something like *The Ring* or *The Grudge*. I do not think in terms of how I am going to scare the shit out of people. To me the zombie films are more like action-adventure, with some shock moments that are meant to slap you in the face. A bit like the operating room scenes in *M*A*S*H*: you laugh at the comedy for two hours, until you stop and realize it is the real world," says this true master of horror.

J. Hoberman once described *Night of the Living Dead* as "the beatnik version of the CBS News." The Vietnam War and "anger about a failed revolution," as Romero puts it, fueled the gruesome, subversive imagery of many a seventies horror film. Similarly, *Land of the Dead* will speak volumes to Jon Stewart's fan base. We live, after all, in an era in which torture, decapitation, and mass graves are a routine feature of the nightly news, and accompanying images are readily available on the Internet. With Romero, John Carpenter, Tobe Hooper, Joe Dante, Larry Cohen, Roger Corman, Dario Argento, and Don Coscarelli working together on a project called *Masters of Horror*, it's possible that the horror genre may indeed be poised to engage with the present moment with renewed depth and vigor.

"I always see the zombies as an external force," says Romero, sitting at a table that's way too small for his imposing frame on the terrace of a French Riviera hotel. "The story is happening around them and nobody is paying attention. The way today nobody is paying attention to things like global warming, or the reason why we Americans are so disliked everywhere else. In my mind, this film was always about ignoring the problem. There is some major shit going on out there, and in a distant way the zombies represent what we, the global community, should really be thinking about: something like . . . power to the people."

Land of the Dead is the first Romero zombie film to sport a studio logo (Universal). Two previous Hollywood experiences, working with mini-major Orion on *Monkey Shines* (1988) and *The Dark Half* (1993), were less than happy. His endings were changed, his ideas twisted. Contractually, he is bound to produce an R-rated cut of *Land*, but so far, he says, despite an extremely tight schedule, things have improved.

Still, it isn't hard to imagine a fat group of Hollywood executives being dismembered and eaten alive in lieu of Dennis Hopper and his pals—and to relish the spectacle. Such is Romero's humor and rage—a roar as potent as Big Daddy's war cry.

George A. Romero Interview

Beth Accomando/2008

Phone interview conducted for KPBS, February 6, 2008. Printed by permission of Beth Accomando, KPBS film critic and author of the blog *Cinema Junkie*.

Beth Accomando: Tell me about the opening shot [of *Diary of the Dead*] with the newscaster and her cameraman. I thought it was very clever. It establishes the first person point of view and it's great the way the anchor blocks our view of the first zombies rising.

George A. Romero: Oh man, I don't know what to say except that it seemed like a good idea at the time. It seemed like a good way to introduce the style and to introduce the whole thematic thing about media and that's of course while the mainstream is still functioning. It's the very first report of these things. And I wanted to have something that I could show again a couple of times later and show how they distorted it and changed it to clean it up. So it seemed like the way to go. You know you get these ideas in the shower. That's really where it came from. It fit the theme of the film and it gave me a device that I could sort of keep using throughout.

BA: And you're the cop that shows up in the re-edited version of that news footage.

GAR: Yeah, I'm the guy that's lying about it. I represent the authority figure that's not telling the truth: "They weren't dead till I made them dead." Part of the reason for doing this film was a throwback; I wanted to go back to a simpler way of doing things, something smaller and more controllable, literally where I had complete control and which I did for the first time since *Night of the Living Dead*. I used to always do a sort of cameo in the first eight of my films. So since we're flashing back in time, I'll do it again.

BA: So was this desire to have more control in part a reaction to having just done *Land of the Dead*, which was a big studio film for you?

GAR: When we did *Land of the Dead* it was Universal and I was sort of terrified going in. I figured, "Oiy, everybody warned me it's terrible working for Universal, they are the Blue Meanies in the Black Tower." And they were great! In the end they really wanted my film. And they let my partner and I make it, make the film we wanted to make, and they were great to work with but it was just a grueling experience making that movie. And still it was guerrilla filmmaking. Even though it was more money than I ever had on a zombie film it wasn't enough money to pull off something that ambitious. So it was just constantly every night compromises. Geez, we didn't get that shot so coming off the set we'd be up for another three hours figuring out what are we going to do tomorrow. It's just grueling. And there was something about it when it got all finished that even though I liked the film a lot, it was like approaching Thunderdome, it was getting a bit too big. I felt that it had out-scaled its origins in a certain sense. When we made the first film we were just a bunch of young people in Pittsburgh making a movie, and I really wanted to get back to that. And I had this idea about doing something about all this emerging media, and I felt that the best way to do that was to go back to the very first night, and tell a parallel story of what happened on the first night of *Night of the Living Dead*. In fact I use some of the news tracks from the original *Night of the Living Dead* in this film to indicate that it's meant to be the same night, the same event. So I felt that was a way to simplify my life and get back to the roots of the series.

BA: Your zombie films have always entailed a lot of social commentary, so what was on your mind this time?

GAR: It occurred to me and still occurs to me that what's happening with this new normal of the media is that everyone is becoming obsessed with the idea of being a reporter and we're invited to—if something happens outside your window—to shoot it and we'll put it on the air. And this blogosphere, which strikes me as being a bit dangerous, I mean there can be some lunatic out there advancing radical ideas, which if they sound at all reasonable, there's all of a sudden a million, two million followers. And it strikes me as dangerous in that it can create more tribalism when it's the last thing we need. I joke but I say if

Jim Jones had thrown up a blog there'd be millions of people drinking Kool-Aid. It bothers me. Plus the fact that people get sucked into it. They think, oh I can be a reporter, I'll take footage of this tornado and I'll get it on the air and maybe I can help. And it's all sort of this feeling that maybe we can help, maybe we can become part of it. It's almost like a new kind of graffiti trying to establish a personal identity. And all of that strikes me as being a bit odd and a bit dangerous. And I wanted to do something about that, so that's where it came from.

BA: The film displays a certain mistrust of the mainstream media, but are you also asking us to distrust your own characters as well? These young student filmmakers who post their videos on the web.
GAR: Oh absolutely! In fact in some ways it doesn't attack the mainstream media. Obviously the mainstream media is being manipulative. What's happening out in the blogosphere is that people think they are helping, but it's little more than opinion, and it's completely uncontrolled. Maybe we're being manipulated and overly managed by the mainstream but that's almost forgivable. I don't know if people are ready to have a million bloggers out there advancing this idea or that point of view. I mean people listen to Limbaugh because they agree with what he says, and what happens with all these blogs is that people who tune into them or become advocates of them, listen to them because they agree with what's being said. And that's what I'm talking about being dangerous. It's absolutely unfettered, uncontrolled, unfettered information, which in most cases isn't even information, it's opinion. And that's the stuff that I feel is dangerous. It's very easy to join up with somebody that you think sounds reasonable, but there might be some radical ideas in there. I'm sure Hitler sounded reasonable to people he spoke to at first.

BA: Talk about how you have a group of student filmmakers making this film. You seem to have some fun with that and deconstructing the whole horror genre.
GAR: Well, I'm taking a few jabs at myself there, and I couldn't help but make a few jokes about fast-moving zombies. I can't resist a little bit of slapstick and humor here and there. So yeah, I was taking a shot at it but it was also a breath of fresh air. The characters in the film reminded me of us when we were making *Night of the Living Dead*. So it was sort of reliving it, kind of nostalgic in a way. I just felt that was the way to do it. That was one of my initial ideas—if I was going to do something

about this, what was the logical way to do it? Well, these film students are out shooting a school project and they have a camera, and so when the zombies begin to walk they just naturally—at least just the one of them at first but then many others, become obsessed with this idea. They just start documenting it. And think they are trying to help and possibly even save some lives. In the meantime, the situation far out-runs everybody. It's really too late to do anything about it.

BA: A lot of films recently have used first-person camera but you made such clever use of the battery dying and the guy being plugged into the wall and not being able to move when he hears screaming, and making us stuck with him unable to see what's going on.

GAR: Well, isn't that the way it would be? I mean that's happened to me shooting home movies and I can't get over to the birthday cake because I have to stay plugged in. Again those are all ideas that come to you in the shower. And I was collaborating with my partner Peter Grunwald, and we had an old friend John Harrison, literally, even sort of the planning of this film sitting around the living room just like the old days, spit-balling ideas and having fun with it. That's really what we set out to do. And that's what we were able to do, and it was great to have enough control to be able to do it. The only thing that when you're working for a studio or when you have a lot of layers of suits between you and the work is you see a sunset and you want to shoot it and you have to write a memo to be able to shoot it. We were able to do anything we wanted to do all the way through post-production. So it was really like going back to the old days.

BA: How do you feel about your film coming out on the heels of *Cloverfield*, a bigger studio film that uses some of the same first-person camera ideas in confronting a disaster? I mean people were calling that independent and experimental.

GAR: You know, I've never been concerned with that. I didn't know about it when we were making our film, but it seems to be that there is a collective subconscious; we had *Redacted*, we have *Cloverfield*, there's *Vantage Point*. I think everyone is noticing, I think it's in the conscious-ness of filmmakers, this idea of "I am a Camera." There are a million cameras out there. I don't know, I'm not a marketing guy. I just made a film that I wanted to make and it's from the heart, and I can't relate it to *Cloverfield*. I almost don't care about it. People have said you can't compare it to *Cloverfield*, then other people have said, well, *Cloverfield* got it wrong and Romero got it right. I don't pay attention to that kind of stuff. There's no way to control it. So all you can do is hope for the best. And my stuff is my stuff. And it's always been sort of me, and if there's anything that I can say I'm proud of is that I've never just sort of taken a job, if you know what I mean. This is an idea that I had and I hope people like it. Obviously on a certain level, *Cloverfield* is this huge thing and we don't need to be competing with it. It's an idea that I had, and happily a lot of people seem to be tuning into it and getting it. And that's enough for me.

BA: Now when you made *Night of the Living Dead* back in the sixties, did you ever think that you'd be able to return to that material repeatedly to find something new?

GAR: Never. I never thought I would do another one. I resisted doing another one for ten years. What happened with *Night of the Living Dead* initially was it went out and played drive-ins and neighborhood theaters and in six months it was gone. But it actually returned some money. It cost us about $115 grand and returned $500,000 to $600,000. We thought okay, that was a nice exercise. And we actually made some bread. I was working on my third film when suddenly the French discovered *Night of the Living Dead*. And began calling it "essential American cinema." I'm going, "Oiy, I didn't know how to make a movie." All I saw were the mistakes in it. And then I almost froze up [and thought] if I'm going to do a sequel or another one, I'm going to have to be as socially conscious, and it became an obsession.

So I waited until I got an idea—the second film was made at a shopping mall. And I met the people who had developed this first big indoor temple to consumerism in western Pennsylvania and it gave me the idea. Then I was trying to be as conscious as I could but I realized I was doing it without innocence. And halfway through that production I sort of shifted gears and said, wait a minute, I can really have fun with this and try to make it reflective of the times, and to make it a comment that doesn't sort of take over the thrill ride part of the film. That's when I developed this sort of conceit, and I waited consciously another ten years to do *Day of the Dead*. And waited until I could reflect again on something different about the times, and the same with *Land*. This one [*Diary of the Dead*] came quicker but I felt I got the idea while we were shooting *Land of the Dead*. And I wanted to do something about this blogosphere. I was actually concerned that people were going to start to do the same thing, and actually it turns out that several people were doing the same thing. So we did it but it grew out of the idea—it didn't come from someone saying, "Hey, make another one, we can make money on it." It wasn't like that at all. The idea came first.

BA: Now at the Comic-Con you said that you had a "balls-out comedy" that you were thinking about as your next zombie film. Is that still true?

GAR: Yes, it's still a possibility. I love it—it literally is a balls-out comedy. It's a completely slapstick idea. Again it would be fun for me, it would almost be like me going on vacation. I'd love to do it, again completely different. It would have nothing to do with any of the other films. It's like *Fido* or *Shaun of the Dead*. It's sort of a sidebar to my zombie films, it just happens to be a film with a zombie in it. A single zombie. I hope someone sees the merit in it and lets me do it.

BA: You said you used audio from the original *Night of the Living Dead* in *Diary*. Talk about the audio because it's quite layered.

GAR: Yeah, it's pretty layered and that's where I was able to get my little messages, my little elbows and asides in the radio and TV broadcast that they are downloading. I had a bunch of buddies that came out to do voice tracks for that. It was really gratifying. I called these guys up and said I need all these news voices, do you want to do one, and everybody said yes. Steve King did one. Tarantino, Wes Craven, Guillermo Del Toro. I mean all my old buddies came out and said, sure man. It was fun and there is much of the message in there and in this narration, which we held off on writing any of it. Our main objective when we were on the set was to get the main action done that involved principle characters. And we were saying to ourselves that these were film students and after they have everything in the can, somebody is going to go and finish this and we can do the same thing. And that's exactly what we did. We had all the principle action in the can and then we came home and started to work on it. I was changing some of those audio tracks until the last couple of days before the film premiered. We were able to work with it like clay. Move the sculpture a little this way, a little that way. That was also the result of having the freedom to do that.

BA: And your film still delivers on the gore, which is quite fun.

GAR: I enjoy it but I was also getting a bit tired of that too. I felt initially that I needed to do it because people wanted it, and I also felt that it was kind of a slap in the face. It's sort of like the operating room sequences in *M*A*S*H*, where you are watching this comedy and laughing your head off, and all of a sudden there's this operating scene, and it just slaps you. It says, guys, there's something to think about here, this is war. That was my sort of rationale for doing it, but again with *Land of the Dead* when you are shooting an objective film with objective cameras, the tendency is to go in and do what I call product shots on the gore. When we were doing this film, I said wait, I think it may be more effective and a little more realistic—because these kids aren't going to go in and do close-ups on the gore—they are going to shoot it from across the room. And I felt that when we started to look at dailies, I thought, wow this is even more effective than going in for a close-up. So it's there and maybe pound for pound it's as much as there is in *Land*, because *Land* was also R rated. But it's like if you were shooting a home movie, it comes and it goes quickly, and it's only viewed from a certain perspective which is way over here across the room and maybe you could zoom in but not that much. It was meant to be through the eyes of the individual cameraman, and I felt it was more effective than going in for all those close-ups.

BA: I wanted to ask, what do you think of today's horror films? Do you like any of them?

GAR: (laughs) Enjoy them? No. I can say that without qualification. I don't understand them. I don't understand this torture porn. I don't get it. I wish someone could give me a reason. I mean it's an angry time so these films are angry. Angry at what? I mean I don't find any political statement in them. I mean when we were angry in the sixties, we were angry at the police, at the military, we were angry at institutions. It strikes me that just being angry isn't enough of a reason to make a cruel film. I've always tried to not make my films cruel. I mean they may be angry but I try to not make them cruel. I try to lighten the load with some humor and all that. I mean being angry is one thing. *Dr. Strangelove* is an angry movie but it's hilarious. So I don't know, I guess I'm more of a traditionalist in that sense.

Turn Me On, "Dead" Man

Peter Keough/2008

Published February 14, 2008. © 2008. *The Boston Phoenix*. Reprinted with permission.
All rights reserved.

Before George Romero (with a nod towards Richard Matheson's 1954 sci-fi novel *I Am Legend*), zombies were just bit (no pun intended) players in the horror genre, inert, usually voodooized automatons that with few exceptions (i.e, Jacques Tourneur's *I Walked With a Zombie* (1943), scheduled for a 2009 remake) left little impression. George Romero made them an icon, indeed, an industry. He also showed the potential of graphic gore. So you might say he's responsible for about 90 percent of the horror industry since 1968 when he made his debut, *Night of the Living Dead*.

Not that he's profited much by it. Though hundreds of millions or more have been made on films inspired by if not directly imitative of his work (including remakes of all of his *Dead* movies to date), he has yet to make a big killing from the property. Maybe it's because he has too much respect for the dead. Each of his *Dead* films aspires to social commentary, even philosophical profundity. His latest, *Diary of the Dead*, is no exception, commenting on a voyeuristic, solipsistic culture of self-devouring media.

Well, let him explain it. I talked with him on the phone last week. As usually happens, I was starting to warm up to some of what I thought were the more interesting questions (Did he think his own films could be responsible for the current fad of torture porn? What would he do if he were indeed president, as a cult T-shirt suggests? What's his cat's name?) when unseen powers cut me dead.

PK: Did you ever have any idea years ago when you made *Night of the Living Dead* that this concept would catch on as it did?
GR: Absolutely not, no, not at all. I was amazed even when the first

163

film . . . You know it was a little film we made in Pittsburgh, a bunch of young people, that, you know, we had a commercial production company, doing beer commercials and industrial films and the like. So we had the equipment and lights and camera and so we tried to make a movie. All the sudden it went out, became a movie, it was *Night of the Living Dead*. Not all of a sudden actually. Initially, you know, it went to drive-ins and neighborhood theaters for six months and then it was gone. We thought that was the end of it. It did return some money, and we were working on our third film before the French discovered it and brought it back from the dead. I resisted doing another one for years until I had another idea. I mean there was such high-minded talk about how it was such a political film, and I was very reluctant to try to tackle another one until I had an idea that was interesting enough, something I wanted to tackle.

PK: Were you worried also, you didn't want to get stuck in the rut of making the same movie all over again?

GR: Yeah, I wasn't so much worried about being stuck in a rut. I love the genre, I grew up on EC comic books and I love doing it. I had this conceit that it would have to be about something, have at least some social satire. It wasn't until I socially knew some people developing this indoor shopping mall around Pittsburgh, that was the first temple to consumerism in the area. That's what gave me the inspiration to do the second film. All of them have been motivated about what's going on in the world, rather than, oh I gotta make another zombie movie.

PK: It seems like every incarnation confronts some kind of topical issue of the time. How would you describe the issue that is behind *Diary of the Dead*?

GR: I just was starting to get concerned, noticing this media explosion, alternate media, the blogosphere and all that, and it just occurred to me that there's some dangers lying here potentially hidden. It just really struck me that this was what was going on in the world now, everyone's a camera, everyone's a reporter, and people seem to be obsessed by it. And you know that tube has a sort of power, and people believe and buy in to what they heard. People that tune in to Rush Limbaugh already know what he's going to say and already agree with him. A lot of these blogs that are going up, the people that subscribe to them are already believers and it strikes me as creating new tribes. It seems to me any lunatic could get on there and suddenly have a following. I've joked about it, if Jim Jones had a blog, we'd have millions of people drinking Kool-Aid. Or if Hitler was around, we wouldn't have to go into the town square; he could just put up a blog. If it sounds at all reasonable to enough people, all the sudden you have all these followers.

PK: There seems to be a conflict between the legitimate media—which you have in the background of all the Dead movies, the TV and radio, which are giving reports and getting more desperate—and then you have the blogosphere or the Internet. Your feelings about both seem to be ambivalent. Can you talk about that?
GR: A bit. The character in the film is obsessed with what he's doing, so obsessed he forgets about his own survival. I find that in the line in the film, if we see a terrible accident we don't stop to help, we stop to look. I'm not ambivalent to that. Maybe he started out well-intentioned but forgetting about your own survival, it's a bit too late to be helpful in that way. It strikes me that everyone is just out there looking for a shot. People are invited too. The set of tornadoes, last night on CNN, they're saying, be careful, but if you can get a good shot, send it in.

PK: They don't want to get paid for it, they just want the notoriety.
GR: Yes, it's a kind of graffiti. I think this whole blogosphere is a kind of graffiti. It's impersonal, identity, some sort of quest for personal identity. The problem is all the sudden people jump on it and a lot of people are listening to you.

PK: On the other hand, it's suggested, at least by the Jason character, that the legitimate media is covering things up. It presents the blogosphere as an alternative way of getting to the truth, and that's his purpose for doing what he's doing.
GR: Yeah, but that's what's happening, right? In the world, there used to be three networks, and everything I'm sure was being controlled and spun. And now there's all this freedom, but now there's no management and it's not even all information, a lot of it is opinion, viewpoint. And I don't know which is worse, I certainly don't have any solution. It strikes me as being one great big muddle. I don't know if people are ready for it. People should take the responsibility to dig into things a little bit but they're very happy to keep on dancing and have a beer and listen to what someone has to say on that tube. And follow along, instead of doing any real investigation, or digging, or finding out about the issues.

PK: So you think it's a culture of hedonistic voyeurs with a short attention span?

GR: Yeah, I think so, for sure. And a perfect willingness to follow whoever stands up and takes the reins.

PK: So it's even more pessimistic than *Land of the Dead* where there's a sense of proletariat uprisings. Are you more pessimistic now than when you made that movie?

GR: I don't know if it's pessimism. I think all of my zombie films are just sort of snapshots of the time they were made; I don't expect them to be much more than that. I guess I have launched some criticism of the way certain things are done, the government, some institutions, but they're really just snapshots of what's going on. And it does strike me as a mess; the whole world just seems to keep chasing its tail and eating itself up by its tail.

PK: I read somewhere that you said the whole Dead series could be seen as a secret history of the country for the past four decades.

GR: Yeah, not so secret. If there's anything that I feel sort of proud of, it's that I've been able to take genre stuff and still sort of express myself a little bit. We do these little snapshots of the era, and I try to do it stylistically with the films as well, I try to make them look like films of that time. And so this one fell right into place that way. The subjective camera and everything. It's part of the collective subconscious these days; everyone seems to be doing it—*Redacted, Cloverfield, Vantage Point*. I think there are several others as well.

PK: You must be a little irritated by *Cloverfield*. You had the idea first—do you feel like they're usurping your notion?

GR: You know it was surprising that someone else was doing it. I didn't think it would necessarily hurt us. I mean that's a big film. I have this niche, we're not competing against that, the four-thousand-screen blockbusters. Again, it's a smaller film. My fans, and those interested in stuff I'm doing will hopefully go out and see it. But you know, I've never felt competitive with the big Hollywood stuff.

PK: This one was a real return to your independent roots.

GR: I wasn't frustrated during the making of *Land of the Dead*, I just saw it getting too big, approaching Thunderdome. It had lost touch with its roots. Its roots were us in the 'Burgh, making a little film. So the characters in this film remind me of us, so there was a certain sort of nostalgia, going back and doing that. But it was also great, working on a low-budget—we only used as much money as we absolutely needed. And I was able to make the film I absolutely wanted to make. Luckily, thanks to the Weinstein company, they thought it would get distributed. Initially, I was ready to knock on doors and try to raise a quarter of a million and shoot this at a film school way under the radar, and then the people at Artfire saw the script and they said, let's do it union, and get a theatrical release. Because of the amount of money involved they gave me the same freedom.

PK: What was the budget?
GR: Under four.

PK: You sort of set it up for a sequel at the end, it looked like.
GR: I mean, not intentionally, maybe there's going to be, since *Night of the Living Dead* all have been set up for sequels with survivors, but I've never done a direct sequel from one to the other. In this case, if it happens, it will be quickly, it probably will be that, continuing on with the same characters. There's a lot more I could say about the emerging media, a lot I didn't get into. You just never know.

PK: It also draws on the first-person shooter games. You get the sense you're going into all these situations where you have to confront them, except with a camera and not a gun—
GR: That's part of it, too. There are times when he's shooting, particularly in the end, why don't you just help him? But he's completely lost in it, to his own downfall.

PK: What do you think of all the remakes that have sprung up over the past decades of your films? All of the Dead films have been remade.
GR: That doesn't give me joy, but I really don't care, I don't have regret. My films are my films. If they want to remake them, that's fine. I've been in interviews with people quoting remakes to me.

PK: Do you get any money from it?
GR: No, not involved at all. In *Dawn of the Dead*, I have a piece of the action there, but it never brings in anything substantial.

PK: You know in the DVD version of that, one of the extras is a video diary of one the survivors. Have you seen that?

[Interrupting publicist]: Sorry! We've got to stop now. We're out of time.

PK: What? We're done?

GR: I'm sorry, I could talk all day . . .

IP: We've got a crazy schedule.

PK: Okay. Thanks.

Interview with George Romero

Peter Keough/2010

Published May 6–8, 2010. © 2010. *The Boston Phoenix*. Reprinted with permission. All rights reserved.

Do a search for the keyword "zombie" on the IMDB and you'll come up with 1,149 titles. Of those some 1,080 have been or will be released since 1968, which was the year George Romero unleashed on the world *Night of the Living Dead*.

Romero himself has contributed his share of these films, all springing from his original, much imitated premise: a plague that reduces its victims to shambling, brain-dead corpses whose only instinct is to eat human flesh and thus create more victims. *Survival of the Dead*, which comes out May 28, is his sixth in the series. I was fortunate to get a chance to talk with the seventy-year-old, very tall, and friendly director about the new movie, the zombie concept, and whether there is any future beyond living death.

PK: You've been busy lately.

GR: Well we've had several screenings. The film premiered at Venice actually and then it was at TIFF and then Texas, Montreal, so it's had festival screenings and then a couple of sort of fan screenings—Vegas and Boston and Texas. And I guess that's what this is tonight, and there was one in Dallas last week.

PK: Is it getting a less fun?

GR: It gets a lot less fun.

PK: Well you got a lot of fans. It must be encouraging to show it to a theater of people who are excited to see a new zombie movie from George Romero?

GR: Good screenings, yeah, when it's a fan screening. The one in Venice was great. It's the first time a genre film has been in competition there since the very first year of Venice and they had *Jekyll and Hyde*, I think. So it was, I think it was getting a big vote, a positive vote from the audience saying we should do more of this, and they were almost trying to convince the committee that they should do more of this. The audience was really just up and howling. I expected to go to Venice and, you know, get the blue-haired ladies.

PK: You've always got a lot of support going back to *Night of the Living Dead* from the Europeans.
GR: Yeah, that's true. But not in Venice. France is much more forgiving of me. Me and Jerry Lewis, I guess. I don't know. So Cannes has always been welcoming; but Venice, never.

PK: Just yesterday we had this emergency that was like one of your movies. You heard about it? The water main broke and people weren't allowed to use the drinking water. They had to boil it first, this went on for like two or three days. I was wondering if this went on for a couple of weeks, it'd be sort of like *The Crazies* or something.
GR: It probably would. I guess so. Once we run out of Poland Spring or whatever.

PK: It doesn't take much to bring the barbarians out.
GR: Yeah.

PK: I talked to you on the phone a while back about *Diary of the Dead* and you said that these movies have been snapshots of the time in society when the film came out. Is *Survival* also a snapshot of these times?
GR: Not so much this time. I mean, *Diary* was. I did it quickly because I felt I had to because it was about emerging media and all that. But this movie exists purely because *Diary* made a lot of money. So I had to sort of reach back and figure out what am I going to do here? So I decided on a much more general theme about war, and then as we were working on this film all this shit started to fly about anger and uncivilized behavior. You know, how we can't disagree without being disagreeable.

PK: And how it seems to have gotten worse since the election of Obama with all the intensified partisanship?

GR: I guess it's a little bit about that. But generally when I first started it's just the whole idea of war, of hatreds that don't die no matter what's going on. And then the second part of the idea was that I said, well, if I have to do this and this film makes money, well then there's going to be another one, and so on. So I decided to take minor characters from *Diary* and take them off on their own adventure and wind up with this little sort of snapshot of what's going on, a little collage of what the world is like three months, six months, eight months later, something like that, a whole new set of films. And then maybe hang it up forever.

PK: I know you made the film before that Arizona law about illegal immigration was passed, but it seemed a weird coincidence that a major theme in the film is violent xenophobia and also that two of the characters are Hispanic. It's kind of like when you had a black actor in *Night of the Living Dead* at a time when racial turmoil was about to break out.

GR: No, I certainly was not talking about Arizona or anything . . . no. When we did *Night*, even with Duane [Jones, the African American actor who played the protagonist], I mean, it wasn't on my mind. We didn't change the script. That script was written with a white guy in mind. He was a truck driver, a redneck kind of guy, and Duane wanted the character to speak more properly and he wanted to . . . he brought all of that. He was worried that he didn't want to look gruff and he wanted to be presentable. He was the one who was much more worried about any of that than we were. We thought, well, it's 1968! We're past all that. In the meantime, you know, rioting in the streets started again and everything else.

PK: Martin Luther King was assassinated around that time, wasn't he?

GR: The night that we finished the film and we were driving the first answer print in the trunk of a car driving to New York to see if anybody, if we could find distribution, on the car radio we heard that Dr. King was shot.

PK: You screened it for a studio on the day Bobby Kennedy was shot, too, right?

GR: I don't remember that story. That might be a Jack Russo [co-screenwriter of *Night*] story, but I don't necessarily remember that.

PK: It was a bad year.

GR: Yeah.

George Romero, Part 2

In which he ponders the meaning of the "zombie walk," why vampires no longer inspire, and other over-analysis.

PK: One of the best vampire movies that I've seen, probably among the top ten, is *Martin* (1977). But you never made another vampire movie after that. Why's that?

GR: I don't know. I haven't been drawn to it. I'm certainly not drawn to it as a . . . even though . . . you know, it's funny, someone today earlier said you did the most popular zombie films as this big critical thing about consumerism and now your zombies have become these consumer items, items that are being consumed and . . . I can't really see it that way. I think video games and graphic novels and things are way more responsible. There's only been one blockbuster zombie movie ever: *Zombieland*, right? I mean, nothing else did more than sixty or seventy [million dollars], I think.

PK: Not *28 Days Later* (2002)? But you say that isn't a zombie movie.

GR: Yeah, but I also don't think that those movies did nearly the box office that *Zombieland* did. I think that it's video games and all of that that are really responsible. I guess zombies are perfect targets for a first-person shooter. But I've never wanted to do vampires just because vampires are cool and hot now. I've never had sort of another idea about doing a vampire film. I don't want to do a vampire movie just to do a vampire movie. And I much prefer this sort of, you know, apocalyptic thing about this. That it's a real game-changer, this thing that's happening with a zombie outbreak and I like that situation much more. Richard Matheson used vampires for that scenario in *I Am Legend* but . . .

PK: You turned them into zombies. Kind of inspired you . . .

GR: It did, yeah, it did . . . I never called them zombies, though. I never thought of them as zombies. In *Dawn* I used the word because everyone was calling them zombies. People started to write about *Night of the Living Dead* and called them "zombies." I said wow, maybe they are. To me they were dead neighbors.

PK: There's a theme that seems to recur and it's directly confronted here, which is the conflict between killing the dead and holding onto the corpse in hopes that they can be restored. Can you talk more about that and why it came to a head in this movie?

GR: It just seemed like a good thing for them to be arguing over and it seemed like an interesting philosophical argument. I mean, I sort of touched on it a little bit in *Day of the Dead* in trying to tame them and trying to keep them around, as functioning. But in this film it just seemed like a really good idea. The guy, the Muldoon character, has a little bit of the holy roller in him and I thought that was a perfect starting place for them. Not a starting place, the argument [between the clans] started over fish and corn way back when, but I thought they would need to have positions on this and it seemed like a good position for them.

PK: They need to have an argument rather than the argument itself being important. Is the religious aspect important to you at all?

GR: It's not super important. I always sort of take a little jab at it whenever I can. I played a priest in *Martin* just to get back at my own confessors when I was growing up. I was raised Catholic and sort of learned early on . . . well, I didn't learn, I just got turned off really pretty quickly . . .

PK: You didn't have any aspirations for a priesthood yourself?

GR: (laughs) Not at all, no, no. Right when they were teaching me, right when the nuns were teaching me that you could be a saint all your life and steal a baseball, get hit by a bus the next moment, you're going to hell. So my grandmother died and while walking home from the funeral home with my uncles and my dad and they said, well, she's in heaven now and I went "not necessarily," and got my ass kicked all over the block.

PK: Are you annoyed when people tend to overanalyze your movies? Are you into that at all?

GR: I'm certainly not into it. I find, oddly, occasionally you come across something and you say, gee, maybe I was thinking that or maybe this does represent that, but most of the time I think a lot of it's just way overanalyzed. To me, the message part of it was all pretty obvious and not underlying. They're almost the theme of the film, zombies are secondary you know, they're sort of like, annoyances. I think maybe it happens because I at least try to do that anyway. It's not just a slasher film, I'm at least trying to put some content in there and the stories are basically people stories. They're not just monster stories in that way. So maybe because of that people are trying to dig for more.

PK: How's this for overanalyzing: the vampire and zombie genres are now popular because of economic reasons, and the zombies are like the working stiffs and the vampires are like elitist parasites.
GR: I think that's a good way of looking at it. I've often said that zombies are the blue-collar monster, but not anymore. Now they can run. It seems like they all joined health clubs.

PK: It seems that there's no shortage of people who want to volunteer to be extras in your movies . . .
GR: Oh, absolutely.

PK: Are there associations of wannabe zombies? Like re-enactors?
GR: I haven't seen that, no. But you know what's stunning to me is the "zombie walks" that have popped up everywhere. Man, I mean, I just did a phoner from Budapest or someplace and they had my voice over a loudspeaker and there were like, three thousand people dressed up like zombies in Budapest. The one in Toronto last year had more than three thousand people. What's that about? I mean, I don't get it. It's sort of an easy makeup job, I guess, for Halloween, but it doesn't always happen on Halloween. What is that about?

PK: Does that disturb you?
GR: It doesn't really. I'm just wondering, you just want to say "get a life." I don't know. I mean, it's great fun. I went to the one in Toronto and it's great and these people are so dedicated. Some of them I wish I could have them on the set, they're so creative. Some of the makeup *is* great, some of the walks and stuff that they do is worthy of Lon Chaney. But *why* is that fun? That's like a, some kind of a new happening. I can't quite identify it.

George Romero, Part 3

On being on the National Guard's ass, remakes, *The Big Country*, and the Irish.

PK: So you do have more Dead movies in the works?

GR: If it happens. I mean, this completely depends on how this film does. If this film performs like *Diary* financially, then they will want another one and I'm ready to do it. I have a really good idea for another one which would take—I don't know if you know *Diary* but there's this black group of looters that used to be National Guardsmen too (I guess I'm on the National Guard's ass) but I'd like to do them. And then I'd like to follow the blond woman that escapes. So I have ideas for them. I don't know whether it's going to happen or not. In the meantime I'm working on another, on a hotter idea which is not zombie, and my partner and I have a script that we're trying to finish which is non-horror. But I don't know. I don't have the energy anymore to go and pitch and take meetings and all that stuff so . . . I'd almost rather do two more of these and call it a day. It's just so tough, you never earn your credit card, your platinum card out in Hollywood, and if you need a bigger budget, you gotta go there, you're not gonna be able to raise it independently.

PK: You have mixed feelings about bigger budgets?

GR: Oh, definitely. I mean, oh boy, if I didn't have to do it, I wouldn't want to. But it's . . . you hit a certain point and everything goes up, you know? The catering, you gotta have stars, you gotta be, you know, everything. From the catering to the trailers.

PK: What was the budget like for this one?

GR: It was about twice what *Diary* was . . . it's whether you're talking American dollars or Canadian dollars, so I'm sort of the wrong guy to talk to. In my mind, *Diary* was around 2.5 US and I think this went to something over 4 US, but in Canada that converts to a lot more because of the rebates that you have. This was a completely Canadian film. They treat you well.

PK: Do you have more CGI effects in this than you do in your other films?

GR: Yeah . . . not necessarily more than *Diary*. Again, when you're shooting, you have to get it in the can in twenty-one days. That's the most expensive time, you just gotta get off the set and if you start screwing around with squibs and everything, you know, a squib blows the wrong way and you gotta clean the wall . . . you know, you lose an hour on an effect that doesn't work and it's just much easier to have the actor point the gun, the other guy falls down, and then you paint the flash in and you paint the splat and you're outta there.

PK: Next to the opening of *The Wild Bunch*, the opening of *Dawn of the Dead* when they raid the apartment building . . . that's gotta be one of the most electrifying pieces of violence on film I've seen.
GR: Wow.

PK: That was all long before CGI
GR: Those were mechanical. Those were all practical, mechanical effects. [Tom] Savini I mean, he did great stuff. And in *Day*, some of the stuff that he pulled off in *Day* was sensational. We used no CG then and I love it, I loved the look of it. I mean, and you know, it acts more with everything, it's—you know, the blood spatter is real. Everything about it is much more real, and the actors, it causes better performances when you're actually tearing something off a guy. So, I much prefer . . . but it just costs you in time. You gotta do it again and you gotta do it again sometimes. You can't do it . . .

PK: Didn't you have like a fifty-dollar special effect challenge that I read somewhere? You challenged people to make a zombie eating effect for fifty dollars?
GR: that may have been some kind of a promotional thing that the distributors did, maybe Weinstein's did that or something, I don't know.

PK: Oh, well somebody did it for twenty dollars.
GR: Well you can, you certainly can. I see these kids . . . what blows me away is how many people, these young people . . . I go to these horror conventions you know, and there must be a dozen kids every time I go that give me a movie that they made and it's finished, they made a box, they did graphics, they did everything on it. Oh, zombie movies! And I keep saying, do something else man! I mean, there's not enough room in the world for three thousand zombie movies.

PK: Do you think your career would be better in some ways if the first movie that you made that was the biggest hit was *Knightriders* (1981), as opposed to *Night of the Living Dead*?
GR: I don't know, I mean, I love *Knightriders*. *Martin* and *Knightriders* are my two favorite films. They're the closest to me. Most personal I think is *Knightriders*. But I don't think it would've been any more suc-

cessful if it was my first film than it was when it came out. I mean, you know, that's the problem with that. Jesus, like everything else, they're talking about remaking that, they're talking about my remaking *Martin* and it just, it drives me nuts . . . *Crazies* got re-made. It's just like, I can't believe it, I sit here and I go, I'm being remade all over the place.

PK: Are you getting rewarded for all this, financially or anything?
GR: The only one was *The Crazies*. They actually paid a fee to use my name as executive producer, and I expected more involvement . . . they just wanted my name on it. But that's the way it goes too. There is a movie of mine that I'd like to remake. I called it *Jack's Wife* (1972) but it had several titles. I would actually like to remake that movie today. I think it would be stronger today. That was sort of my women's lib movie, and I don't think I was quite sensitive enough to it when I made the film. I still think it's okay, it's not terrible, but no money and no cast . . . I don't mean big cast, the acting wasn't so good. I'd like to remake that one.

PK: *Survival* has kind of a Western feel, have you always wanted to make a Western? This is sort of your compromise?
GR: It's never been a passion, no. I love certain old Westerns and obviously this was . . . I don't know if I mentioned but *The Big Country* is what we decided, I got all the department heads together and showed them *The Big Country* (1958) and said, "Let's do this," and we decided to go all the way with 2:35 [aspect ratio] and not mute the colors and you know, try to make it look a little Wyler-esque or whatever but . . . that was just fun, that was indulgence.

PK: Where did the Irish accents come from?
GR: The two actors, basically. I mean, I called them O'Flynn and Muldoon but they were both . . . Kenny Welsh is noted for his Irish characters that he's played and the other guy, I think Richard Fitzpatrick is Irish . . . I don't know, I don't think Welsh is Irish but Richard Fitzpatrick is, so they both decided to really lay it on.

PK: The Irish are known for their tribalism . . .
GR: Well it was okay with me because I said you know, if you want to think of this as Ireland or the Middle East or whatever, but Ireland was in there, one of the places where this happens, where it has happened in the past.

George A. Romero on *Survival of the Dead*

Tony Williams/2010

Interview conducted July 5, 2010. Previously unpublished.

Q: You've mentioned that William Wyler's *The Big Country* (1958) inspired you for the depiction of the warring O'Flynn and Muldoon patriarchs in *Survival of the Dead*. Why did you choose to insert elements of the western into this film?

A: After I made *Land of the Dead*, which was the fourth of the zombie films, I was very comfortable with doing these "ten years apart" episodes reflecting the decades in which they were done and having fun with that. Basically, I'm being playful. I have this identifiable routine that I'm able to get away with to express myself and my opinions within this particular genre, one that unfortunately is not frequently used enough for that kind of thing. Even when we were still shooting *Land of the Dead*, I had this idea of wanting to do something about emerging media such as citizen journalism. So I started to work on a script. When I finished *Land*, I completed the script for *Diary of the Dead*.

I didn't like the way *Land* was distributed. It was the first time I'd made such a film on a big budget with studio involvement and I don't think they took it seriously enough. I was upset with the amount of work and everything that went into that. So I thought, "Maybe I could make this little film for a million bucks from some independent source." It would be like a vacation to have some form of control again. Artfire were willing to make that deal with us so it was done very quickly. The way I structured it was the idea of shooting a student film when the whole thing happened so I couldn't continue the saga. I had to go back to the first night. What's wrong with that? Other people have done it! So we made *Diary* and I thought it was going to be a stand-alone film. But because it was so inexpensive and gained a limited studio release, it ended up making a lot of money from DVD and European release. So Artfire said, "Let's make another one." *Diary* was the first one I'd made

178

very quickly after *Land*. So I was suddenly faced with making another one. It was either "You do it" or "We do it." So I chose to do it. So I said, "What if I make this one and it makes a lot of money? Are you going to ask me to make another?"

This is a very long way around this answer, but it shows you how *Survival* happened. I laid the groundwork for a series of films based around characters that had played minor roles in *Diary*. So we'll have this trilogy or four films, whatever it turns out to be. For the first time we'll control them. They won't be in the hands of a million other people. So I developed this idea around the National Guard guys from *Diary* and another story idea involving the African Americans the students met at a warehouse as well as one featuring the blonde woman who gets away. *Survival* represented the first idea that I decided to do. Also being slightly bored even though I loved the script, I got together with my director of photography and production designer and said, "How can we have more fun with this? What if we do each of these films in a different and traditional style?" I had the idea of these feuding guys from *The Big Country*. So I got together with everyone, especially the wardrobe designers and watched a print of the film suggesting "Why don't we try to make *Survival* look like that stylistically?" So that's it. It's quite whimsical and more fun for us. I did think it helped and made *Survival* more timeless, giving it a wonderful flavor and it turned out to be great fun for us. "We're making a movie—a real, old fashioned movie!" That's a long answer but that's what happened.

Q: Do I detect a John Ford influence not only in the Irish element but the final battle being your version of *The Gunfight at the O.K. Corral*? In *My Darling Clementine* (1946), Wyatt states specifically that the confrontation is to be a family affair.
A: If I had anything in mind it was *The Big Country*. I love those movies but I don't pretend to be Ford. I wish I had an idea that was worthy enough, and I don't know enough about American history so I have to say no.

Q: Were you familiar with other films merging the western with horror such as *Curse of the Undead, Billy the Kid vs. Dracula,* and *Jesse James Meets Frankenstein's Daughter*?
A: You've left out *Valley of the Gwangi*! No, I wasn't even thinking on those terms. I was thinking of doing *Survival* stylistically like a western. The characters were going to an island. We won't show any cars so we'll

drop them back in time visually, put others in western costume and suggest this even though it's never stated.

Q: Why did you shoot *Survival* in 2.35 ratio?
A: Because of *The Big Country*.

Q: Most commentators have noticed that this is the first time you've ever repeated a character with Sarge. But Devon Bostick (listed as "Boy") in the credits does not appear to be Brian from *Land of the Dead*.

A: He's a different character. The other thing that intrigued me about wanting to do a collection of small films based on characters in *Diary* is the fact that if you read enough Stephen King novels you come to know every individual character who lives in Castle Rock. King's been able to build a mythology, but because I don't have any control or ownership of my previous films I've never been able to do that. So I'd like to be able to say that because Alan Van Sprang appears as Brubeck in *Land* that it is the same guy. Maybe in my mind it is but legally I can't say that.

Q: Where exactly was Plum Island in Ontario?
A: Just about forty miles away from Toronto. We hired an aerial photographer to shoot islands off Nova Scotia and we picked one of the islands. But everything else was shot inland.

Q: Why did you decide to populate Plum Island with two Irish families who appear to be first generation?
A: Again, I don't know. I didn't think it would be believable to make one Arab and the other Jewish!

Q: *Survival* is obviously an expansion of one sequence in *Diary* where the older couple attempts to protect their zombie children from the military.
A: Yes, I've often used such ideas. People say to me, "All of a sudden your zombies are getting smart, driving cars and riding horses" and I reply, "Did you see any of my other movies?" I've employed such ideas often. Maybe I'm advancing them too much if *Survival* is a few months later than *Diary*. But it's funny how people don't notice what goes on in the other films. I don't think what happens in *Survival* violates any of the rules. If I get to do·more films, I have in my hip pocket the theme

of the zombies eating the horse since none of the characters in *Survival* knows this happened. So that's going to be a surprise for any character in the future if it comes to that. I've played with the same themes over and over and I keep getting away with it.

Q: What made you decide to use the idea of twin daughters in the film?
A: Again, I think it was a neat plot device and repeated the idea of sameness, namely that the zombies are really us. What better way than to have the same person and someone we think is the same person but one is dead and the other isn't. It's one of those instinctive things that came to me. Father comes back and thinks his daughter is dead. Also, it offers us that little shock. They're us and we're them!

Q: Are we to understand that, like Muldoon, O'Flynn can not bear to kill his zombie daughter Jane?
A: When O'Fynn first sees Jane riding her horse he thinks it is Janet and doesn't have a chance to kill her. Sarge has him on the ground. We think it's Janet so he doesn't have a chance to do anything. We don't know if he will. But O'Flynn does shoot Janet at the end. That's a plot cheat. We don't know when Jane died so at the back of my mind I assumed that O'Flynn didn't have a chance to kill her. But he does shoot Janet. What a great actor Kenny Welsh is.

Q: Yes. Again, you cast everybody so well and who needs highly paid stars when you can get great performances out of these actors.
A: I've been hoping that people will agree. That was the other thing about *Land*. It was a Universal production so I got stars such as Dennis Hopper and Asia Argento, so I thought "Let's see if it matters" and it didn't. But even though I liked *Land* I was disappointed. I thought it a big "Who needs it?" if you have good collaborators and suits are all around and all that. I wasn't allowed to use Adam Swica to shoot *Land* because he didn't have a Universal credit! It was so frustrating because he is a wonderful cinematographer. He shot *Diary* and *Survival*. He's a great director of photography and a wonderful friend. It's good to work with a friend because start-up costs are high in any relationship. It's only the people who fund movies for a living who don't understand the personal relationships involved. "I want a guy with a Universal credit"!

Q: *Survival* certainly echoes the 1970s family horror films with Janet having "issues" with her father, as Sarge notes, and the two warring patriarchs.
A: In "many" ways! I wish you could have seen the first cut of their initial confrontation in the film. I ran wild with the dialogue. That scene was originally twelve pages long and you wound up slicing and cutting. That's the hardest thing.

Q: As with Ben and Harry in *Night of the Living Dead*, O'Flynn and Muldoon are rigid and refuse to compromise. They both have solutions that work in particular cases but also act in irrational and contradictory ways.
A: Thank you for noticing. As for other viewers I feel, "What are you going to do?"

Q: I like the scene where Tomboy almost chokes on the food prepared by Muldoon's zombie wife chained in the kitchen. Was this an ironic dig at the blinkered attitude of someone who eats anything, even bad zombie cooking?
A: He eats it avidly and digs right in!

Q: Janet is too late to tell the survivors that Muldoon's experiment worked. Was this an echo of *The Crazies* where the scientist's successful experiment also comes to nothing due to the intervention of fate?
A: I keep using the same devices and if they work I keep using them.

Q: I noticed an irony in the scene where Boy offers Janet a million dollars and then there is a lap dissolve to the zombies in the corral, suggesting that living and dead appear dominated by dead values. Was this intentional?
A: No. I see what you are pointing at. I always thought that scene was a little too much. It was a bit of a device where I just wanted to show that Boy caught up with Janet and that they both returned. I didn't want them to just show up so I thought that, at least, I could throw this little moment in there where he tempts her, but I think that was a bit too much. The thing with the money served a purpose. But I wish I could go back and do something better with it.

Q: Usually, zombies never fight each other in your films. But *Survival* ends with a gunfight between O'Flynn and Muldoon clicking empty chambers at each other with a giant moon (significantly a dead planet) in the background. This is a very bleak and ironic ending.

A: I hope so! (laughs) It's an album jacket, right? I thought, "Why not?" I guess you're right. My zombies have never gone up against each other, but I felt that their behavior was so ingrained like driving a car. These guys just know they hate the other guy and try to kill him. Their chambers are empty and so are they!

Q: The use of a Canadian talk-show host watched by Kenny on his laptop computer is another of your digs against the media. What led you to feature this person in particular?

A: I've often used this kind of thing. In my original draft I made a lot more of that. The host and guest were supposed to be the last guys on the air and really pretend talk-show guys, but I didn't have time to develop the idea and it would have taken too long.

Q: Did you see the O'Flynn and Muldoon feud representing contemporary American politics such as the Democrats and Republicans at loggerheads and destroying themselves as well as the country?

A: You could look at it that way. I did think of that. Peter and I talked about it a lot. It could also represent Israel and the Middle East or the Senate. The whole world needs an anger management plan. In my mind you could take it whatever way you want. It's the same kind of irrational behavior. "I don't remember what started this fight. But I'm on this side and I don't like you!"

Q: Do you have any plans for making a non-zombie film in the future like *The Crazies*, *Jack's Wife*, and *Knightriders*, or will you still continue to explore the world of zombies?

A: As I mentioned we have these new zombie ideas but I've also been working with some people on a video game where zombies are not fast moving! Right now, I'm working on a script that needs to be a horror film because it's me and everybody will want it to be a horror film. To me, its more psychological, a non-zombie scary thriller.

Q: I hope Peter will allow you to do *The Golem* sometime.

A: I keep saying to him, "Yes, let's crack it!" Peter is Jewish. Every idea I come up with he says, "It's too Jewish!"

Index